Bristol

a pocket miscellany

Sarah Coles

First published 2011

The History Press
The Mill, Brimscombe Port
Stroud, Gloucestershire, GL5 2QG
www.thehistorypress.co.uk

British Library Cataloguing in Publication Data.
A catalogue record for this book is available from the British Library.

ISBN 978 0 7524 5976 9

Typesetting and origination by The History Press
Printed in Great Britain

Coat of Arms

The meaning of the motto *Virtute Et Industria*
is 'virtue and hard work'.

*

A ship and castle, signifying strongly fortified harbour.

*

A shield, which was in use from the fourteenth century.

*

Two supporting unicorns were added in 1569 as well
as the crest of two arms rising from the clouds holding
scales and a serpent.

*

The significance of the imagery: unicorns will only do homage
to men of virtue; the arms in the crest signify that good
government depends on wisdom (the serpent) and justice
(the scales) and that these are divine gifts from above.

Contents

Bristol

Pronounced Bris-stall
(or old English Brycgstow)

Means 'the place at the bridge'.

Grid Reference

Ordnance Survey grid ref: ST 59001 72909
(OS Map, 1946)

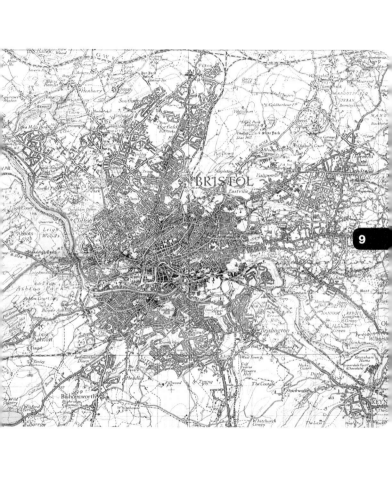

Earliest Appearance on a Map

Bristol appears variously as 'Bristoll du' and 'Bristollu' on three of four maps of Great Britain designed by Matthew Paris in around 1250.

Bristol also appears as 'Bristowe' on the 'Gough Map' of Great Britain, AD 1360.

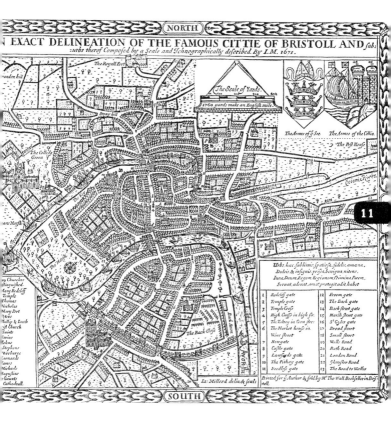

AN EXACT DELINEATION OF THE FAMOUS CITTIE OF BRISTOLL AND *suburbs thereof Composed by a Scale and Ichnographically described. By I.M. 1671.*

The Royall Fort

The Scale of Yards

1760 yards make an English mile.

The Armes of ⌗ See.   The Armes of the Cittie.

The Pest House

Froome River

The Colledg Green

Mary Marsh

Strong hill

Brandon hill

The Marsh

The Back Close

Redcliff hill

BROAD

11

*Urbs hæc sublimi spatiosa, fidelis, amæna,
Dulcis & insignis prisca benigna nitens.
Iura, Deum Regem, Regionem Crimina vincens,
Servat, adorat, amat, protegit odit, habet.*

1	Redcliff gate	12	Froom gate
2	Temple gate	13	The Back gate
3	Temple Cross	14	Back street gate
4	High Crosse in high str.	15	Marsh street gate
5	The Tolzey in Corn str:	16	St Gyles gate
6	The Market house in	17	Broad street
7	Wine street	18	Small street
8	Newgate	19	Wells Road
9	Castle gate	20	Bath Road
10	Lawfords gate	21	London Road
11	The Pithay gate	22	Glocester Road
	Reedlesse gate	23	The Road to Welles

Churches distinguished
Mary Redcliff
Temple
Thomas
Mary Port
Peter
Phillip & Iacob
[...] Church
Saints
Iohns
Stephens
Werburge
Leonards
Iames
Michaels
Augustins
Gaunts Cathedrall

Ia: Millerd delin & sculp

Printed for ⌗ Author & sold by Mr Tho: Wall Bookseller in Bristoll.

Street Names

Name changes:
Christmas Steps was **Knyfesmyth Street**
Wine Street was **Wynch Street**
Arley Hill was **Lampblack Hill**
Narrow Plain and Broad Plain were **St Philip's Plain**
Lower Park Row was **Griffin Lane**

Plus:
Albert Road x 5 – BS2, 15, 16, 20 & 31 – which has potential to cause great confusion when ordering a takeaway.

Badger Sett, St George BS5.

Catbrain Hill, BS10.

Dings Walk, BS2.

East Shrubbery, Redland BS6 – also West Shrubbery and Shrubbery Cottages which all envelop a central shrubbery.

Feeder Road, BS2 – one of many roads feeding the traffic through the city by the waterside.

George and Dragon Lane, BS5 – runs close by its namesake public house.

Hotwell Road, BS8 – running through the area of Hotwells, this road is often mistakenly given an incorrect 's'.

Isambard Walk, BS1 – named after the engineering genius Isambard Kingdom Brunel, who gave Bristol the Suspension Bridge, Temple Meads Station and the SS *Great Britain*.

Johnny Ball Lane, BS2.

Keg Store, BS1.

Leicester Square, Soundwell BS16 – with not quite as many cinemas as its London namesake.

Marlborough Hill, BS2 – well-known locally as 'heart attack hill' due to its extreme steepness.

Newfoundland Circus, Road, Street and Way, BS2 – all in honour of John Cabot's discovery in 1497.

Owls Head Road, BS15.

Pitch and Pay Lane, BS6.

Queen Square, BS1 – completed in 1727, a magnificent Georgian square and once a fashionable residential address. Now mainly offices.

Raja Rammohun Roy Walk, BS16.

Stepping Stones, BS4.

There and Back Again Lane, BS8.

University Close, Hall, Road and Walk – BS8 & BS9.

Victoria Square, Clifton BS8 – with a house in one corner where Queen Victoria once stayed.

Welsh Back, BS1 – once an important street for coastal trade.

York Place, BS8 – Georgian terrace in Clifton, which, in the past, was famed for its York Café, a favourite with students.

Zed Alley, off Host Street, BS1.

Bristol Ward Snapshots

Ashley – Contains the areas of Ashley Down, Baptist Mills, Montpelier, St Andrews, St Pauls and St Werburgh's.

Avonmouth – Port and suburb on the Severn Estuary at the mouth of the River Avon.

Bedminster – South of the River Avon and very heavily bombed during the Second World War.

Bishopston – Situated around the Gloucester Road in the north of the city.

Bishopsworth – Contains the areas of Bedminster Down, Highridge and Withywood.

Brislington, East & West – Contains the areas of Broomhill, St Anne's Park, Arnos Vale, Kensington Park and St Anne's.

Cabot – Gets its name from Cabot Tower and includes the docks, the city centre and the University of Bristol.

Clifton – Contains the areas of Cliftonwood and Hotwells. One of the oldest and most affluent areas, much of it having been built with profits from tobacco and the slave trade.

Cotham – Affluent, leafy inner-suburb situated between Clifton and St Pauls.

Easton – Inner-city area including Lawrence Hill, Whitehall and Barton Hill. The Bristol & Bath Railway Path passes through it.

Eastville – In the central north of the city, home to Eastville Park with its lake.

Filwood – South of the city centre and includes Filwood Park, Lower Knowle and Inns Court.

Frome Vale – Includes the suburbs of Fishponds and Frenchay.

Hartcliffe – Construction of this estate on the edge of the city began in 1952 and Imperial Tobacco once had offices and a factory here.

Henbury – Five miles north west of the city centre and formerly a village in Gloucestershire.

Hengrove – Situated between Whitchurch, Knowle and Bishopsworth.

Henleaze – To the north of the city centre and mostly developed in the 1920s.

Horfield – Remained largely rural until the early nineteenth century.

Kingsdown – Central residential area north of the city centre and south of Cotham.

Knowle – In the south of the city bordered by Filwood Park, Brislington, Whitchurch and Totterdow.

Lockleaze – Long, narrow residential area three miles north of the city centre.

Montpelier – North Bristol with its own railway station and an 'alternative' reputation.

Redland – Affluent suburb between Clifton, Cotham, Bishopston and Westbury Park. Popular student accommodation area.

Sea Mills – Three miles north-west of the city centre, towards the seaward end of the Avon Gorge near Shirehampton.

Southmead – Northern suburb, where the River Trym rises and flows southwest through Badock's Wood nature reserve.

Southville – Inner-city area south of the River Avon. It was the centre for the tobacco and tanning industries.

St George, East and West – East Bristol including Burchell's Green, Crew's Hole and Two Mile Hill.

Stockwood – Residential area in south Bristol.

Stoke Bishop – Affluent area in north-west Bristol including Sneyd Park and most of the Downs.

Totterdown – South of the city centre, it rises steeply from the river bank. Largely terraced Victorian houses, many of which are brightly painted.

Westbury-on-Trym – In the north of Bristol, it retains a village atmosphere.

Windmill Hill – In the south of the city and is often referred to as being part of Bedminster.

Distance From...

Place	Km	Miles
Ayers Rock, Northern Territory	15,641	9,720
Brussels, Belgium	486	302
Centre of the Earth	6,357	3,950
Death Valley	8,310	5,164
Eiffel Tower, Paris	888	552
Frankfurt, Germany	1,176	730
Guernsey, Channel Islands	222	138
Hong Kong	9,768	6,070
Isle of Man	336	209
Jerusalem	3,763	2,338
The Kremlin, Moscow	2,654	1,649
London Eye	170	106
The Moon (average distance) (NB: varies by 23,000km due to elliptical orbit)	384,404	238,857
The North Pole	4,103	2,976
Osaka, Japan	9,596	5,962
The Panama Canal	8,349	5,188
Queenstown, SA	17,387	10,804
Reykjavik, Iceland	1,803	1,120
The Sun (NB: varies by 5,000,000km due to elliptical orbit)	149 million	93 million
The Taj Mahal	7,044	4,377
Ural Mountains (Yekaterinburg)	4,005	2,489
Vatican City	1,558	968
Washington DC	5,734	3,563
Xanthi, Greece	2,379	1,478
Yellowstone National Park	7,090	4,405
Zurich	922	573

Statues

William III, bronze by Bysbrack, Queen Square.

Neptune, Quay Head.

Queen Victoria by Joseph Edgar Boehm, edge of College Green, marble

Edward Colston by John Cassidy, in Colston Avenue, bronze.

Edmund Burke, MP for Bristol 1774-1780, in Colston Avenue, bronze.

Samuel Morley, MP for Bristol 1868-1885 by J. Havard Thornes, Lewin's Mead.

King Edward VIII by Henry Poole, outside the Victoria Rooms on Queens Road.

John Wesley, eighteenth-century Methodist preacher by C.A. Walker, 1933, forecourt of Wesleyan chapel known as the New Room in Broadmead.

John Cabot by Stephen Joyce, 1985, by Bush House on Narrow Quay, bronze.

Isambard Kingdom Brunel by John Doubleday, outside Osborne Clarke offices in Temple Back East.

Raja Rammohun Roy by Niranjan Pradhan, in front of Central Library on College Green.

William Tyndale, New Millennium Square.

William Penn, New Millennium Square.

Thomas Chatterton, New Millennium Square.

Cary Grant, New Millennium Square, bronze.

Elizabethan Seaman/Merchant Venturer, entrance to Council House, College Green, Portland stone.

Cloaked Horseman, on site of old St Bartholomew's Hospital, not far from Whitefriars, St Bartholomew's House.

Sabrina, Goddess of the Severn by Gerald Laing, courtyard of Broad Quay House.

Refugee by Naomi Blake, dedicated to victims of racial prejudice, in the garden at the rear of the Cathedral. It can be glimpsed through the gate on Trinity Steps.

Baltic Wharf Sculptures x 3, themed to link to maritime nature of the area.

Spirit of Bristol by Paul Mount, close to St James Barton roundabout, polished metal.

Exploration, Redcliff Quay.

Castle Park, various statues and sculptures.

Samuel Plimsoll (1824-1898), campaigned to protect seamen who at the time could be fined and sent to prison if they refused to sail in unsafe (overloaded) ships. A bust is on the Avon river side of Hotwells, set beside the entrance to Bristol Docks.

Twinnings

Beira, Mozambique
Developed from the Anti-Apartheid movement in the '80s, the Bristol-Beira partnership has been established with the aim of promoting lasting peace and development.

Bordeaux, France
Twinned with Bristol in 1947, it is estimated more than 30,000 have taken part since the Bordeaux exchange started. Bristol bands and performers take part in the Fête du Fleuve in front of tens of thousands of Bordelais.

Guangzhou, China
The Bristol China Partnership was founded in 1998, and the partnership places a tremendous amount of emphasis on establishing and developing educational links between schools in Bristol, Guangzhou and the wider Guangdong Province.

Hanover, Germany
Twinned with Bristol since 1947. In 2010 there was a scouting exchange between the cities, a cathedral choir tour and a visit from the Ariel rowing club to Hanover, who have been part of the sporting exchange which has lasted for thirty years.

Oporto, Portugal
Twinned in 1984, the cities share many characteristics; they are of similar size, both are Atlantic ports, significant centres of manufacture and regional capitals.

Puerto Morazan, Nicaragua
Set up in 1985 in order to promote solidarity with Nicaragua and to enable communities to benefit from cultural, educational and commercial exchange.

Tbilisi, Georgia
Bristol and Tbilisi became twinned cities in 1988 when Georgia was still firmly part of the Soviet Union. The twinning between the cities was kept alive during the first fifteen years by a small group of enthusiasts because of economic turmoil in the Soviet Union.

International Bristols

Bristol, England is not alone in the world. There is a Bristol in:

Bristol, Iowa, Worth County, United States
Bristol, State of Indiana, Elkhart County, United States
Connecticut, Hartford County, United States
Maryland, Anne Arundel County, United States
Michigan, Lake County, United States
New Hampshire, Grafton County, United States
Pennsylvania, Bucks County, United States
Rhode Island, Bristol County, United States
State of Georgia, Pierce County, United States
State of Illinois, Kendall County, United States
State of Louisiana, United States
State of Maine, Lincoln County, United States
State of New York, Ontario County, United States
State of Nevada, Lincoln County, United States
State of Ohio, Morgan County, United States
State of Washington, Kittitas County, United States
Vermont, Addison County, United States
Virginia, City of Bristol, United States
West Virginia, Harrison County, United States

Alsace, Departement du Haut-Rhin, France
Costa Rica
Departamento de Loreto, Peru
Jamaica
Manitoba, Canada
Quebec, Canada

Historical Timeline

First evidence of
Bristol from a tenth-
century coin.

Wellington defeats
Napoleon at Waterloo.

Clifton Suspen:
Bridge opens.

Bristol becomes
primary slaving port.

SS *Great Britain*
is launched.

1000 AD **1736** **1815** **1843** **186(**

1699 **1807** **1833** **1859**

Population of
Bristol c. 25,000.

Victoria crowned Queen.

Charles Darwin's
*On The Origin of
Species* published.

Slave trade abolished.

Worldwide flu epidemic.

Replica of *The Matthew* sails to Newfoundland.

Bristol City FC founded.

Bristol Airport, Lulsgate opens.

1894   **1919**   **1957**   **1997**

83   **1909**   **1932**   **1964**   **2003**

.stol Rovers founded.

First edition of the *Bristol Evening Post.*

Concorde's last flight.

Bristol University founded.

The Beatles play the Colston Hall.

Bristol Cathedral Then and Now

Seasons

Highest temperatures:
2000-2010: 33C, August 2003.
1990-2000: 35C, August 1995.

Lowest temperatures:
2000-2010: -8C, January 2010.
1900-2000: -10C, January 1982.

Wettest month:
2000-2010: 271mm, November 2009.
1900-2000: 258mm, September 1918.

Snowiest year:
2009-10.
1962-63.

Windiest day:
January 2007, gusts of up to 68mph.
January 1990, gusts of up to 91mph.

Worst floods:
1889, as a thick blanket of snow thawed.
October 1882: 3ft of rain fell.
1703: great storm that submerged half of Bristol.

2010 was the coldest start to January in Bristol for twelve years – temperatures fell as low as -8 degrees centigrade.

Average temperature from 8.2C in 1853 to 11.3C in 2009 – 3.1 degree rise in 156 years.

Average daily January temperature: 7C / 45 degrees F.
Average daily July temperature: 22C / 72 degrees F.

Average rainfall from 73.5mm in 1970 to 103.5mm in 2000 – 30mm rise in thirty years.

24-Hour Timeline

The major theatres and concert venues – Old Vic, Hippodrome, Colston Hall – have emptied their auditoria for another day.

The bus station in Marlborough Street begins its busy stream of vehicles transporting people around the city

The first flights leave Bristol airport.

Bristol Cathedral opens its doors to visitors and worshippers.

Cabot Circus opens its doors to shoppers.

0000   0500   0630   0800   1000
**   0200   0600   0730   0930   12(**

Nightclubs begin to reach turning out time.

Bristol Ferry begins daily operations around the docks.

In the summer College Green Queen Square with students a workers enjoy their lunches.

Birds all around the city begin their dawn chorus.

Market traders at St Nicholas Market on Corn Street start trading.

30

andwich shops
nd coffee bars
ll around the
ity are heaving
vith hungry
vorkers.

Shops start to close and the
evening rush hour of buses,
bicycles and cars begins.

Restaurants begin to
empty of sated diners.

Penguin feeding
time at Bristol Zoo.

Weary commuters
make their way home
across the city from
Temple Meads station.

1300   1500   1700   2000   2200 . . .
1400   1600   1900   2100

School runs collecting
children cause traffic chaos
throughout the city suburbs.

Jazz kicks off at
the Old Duke in
King Street.

During the school holidays,
Bristol Packet boat leaves
Wapping Wharf and cruises
around the docks and river
serving cream teas.

Curtain up for
numerous theatre
performances
city-wide.

How Many Times a Year?

9 million tourists visit Bristol each year.

Cumberland Basin swing bridge swings approximately 800 times a year (opened in 1965 as Plimsoll Bridge).

Up to 438,000 vehicles cross the Clifton Suspension Bridge every year.

182,500,000 car movements every year in and out of the city centre.

At All Saints' Church, Corn Street, two carved and painted figures swing out and chime every quarter of an hour – a total of 35,040 times per year.

Clifton Suspension Bridge is not painted every year – it is painted once every 5-10 years depending on weather and budget.

The lights on Clifton Suspension Bridge are not light bulbs that need changing numerous times each year – they comprise 3,000 LEDs which should last at least 15-20 years.

Broad Street Then and Now

St Mary Redcliffe Then and Now

Demographics

Population: 443,100 (2008 census)
Projected to reach 519,800 by 2026
England's sixth – and the United Kingdom's
eighth - most populous city.

Size: 42.5 square miles, 110 square kilometres.

Number of full-time students living in Bristol during term time:
25,600.

Black and minority ethnic residents: 11.9 per cent.

One-person households: 33.3 per cent.

Unemployment rate: 6.4 per cent.

Residents qualified to degree level: 34.5 per cent.

People working in Bristol city centre: 91,100 .

Children (under 16): 19.2 per cent (1991 census).

Proportion of young adults (16-24) who were lone parents:
2.4 per cent (1991 census).

Pensionable age (over 65): 19.4 per cent, increase of 0.8 per
cent since 1981 (1991 census).

TRAMWAY CENTRE
BRISTOL. 14

Bristol Panoramas

Quotations from Literature

'Nine days I floated starving, and a negro lass beside,
Till for all I tried to cheer her, the poor young thing she died;
But as I lay a gasping a Bristol sail came by,
And brought me home to England here to beg until I die.'
The Last Buccaneer, Charles Kingsley

'True, and then as to her manner; upon my word I think it is
particularly graceful, considering she never had the least
education; for you know her mother was a Welsh milliner,
and her father a sugar-baker at Bristol.'
The School for Scandal, Richard Brinsley Sheridan

'True; who bears hard
His brother's death at Bristol, the Lord Scroop.'
King Henry IV Part I, Shakespeare

'I'll put one to that,' cried the old mahogany-faced seaman –
Morgan by name – whom I had seen in Long John's public-house
upon the quays of Bristol. 'It was him that knowed Black Dog.'
Treasure Island, Robert Louis Stevenson

'Well, to make a long story short, we got a few hands on board, made
a good cruise home, and the HISPANIOLA reached Bristol just as
Mr Blandly was beginning to think of fitting out her consort.'
Treasure Island, Robert Louis Stevenson

Quotations From Famous People

'The Bristol Channel was always my guide, and I was always able to draw an imaginary line from my house over in Wales. It was a great comfort.'
Roald Dahl

'There are bad times just around the corner, we can all look forward to despair, it's as clear as crystal, from Bridlington to Bristol, that we can't save democracy, and we don't much care.'
Noel Coward

'I'm a Bristol person too. I lived in Bristol during the war.'
Julian Glover

'Beneath this east river drive of the city of New York lie stones, bricks and rubble from the bombed city of Bristol in England. These fragments that once were homes shall testify while men love freedom to the resolution and fortitude of the people of Britain. They saw their homes struck down without warning… it was not their walls but their valour that kept them free.'
Plaque unveiled in New York following a speech by Bristol man Cary Grant

Famous for...

Bristol Blue Glass
Around for hundreds of years, the special blue hue comes from the cobalt oxide inside. It was possibly popularised by Bristol's wealthy merchants, who were drawn to its unusual colour.

Harvey's Bristol Cream
A brand of Spanish sherry bottled in Bristol since 1796 by John Harvey & Sons. The name comes from a visitor who once compared it to ordinary milk, with the delicious drink, in comparison, the cream.

Wallace & Gromit and Aardman Animations
A world leader in animation, and the producers of Oscar-winning films starring Wallace and his dog, Gromit.

John Cabot
Italian explorer whose 1497 discovery of parts of North America began aboard the famous ship *The Matthew.*

Cabot Tower
A 30m tall red sandstone tower built in 1897 to mark the 400th anniversary of Cabot's first voyage. There is another in Newfoundland.

Cary Grant
Real name Archibald Leach, one of the most famous Bristol men.

Brunel
Famous engineer Isambard Kingdom Brunel gave Bristol the wonderful Clifton Suspension Bridge, and also the SS *Great Britain.*

Banksy
Whether loved or loathed, this now iconic artist's pieces cannot be ignored.

International Balloon Fiesta, and International Kite Festival
Both free to attend, these fabulous festivals attract up to 500,000 visitors to the city.

Infamous for...

Slavery

Between 1697 and 1807, 2,108 known ships left Bristol to make the trip to Africa and onwards across the Atlantic with slaves. Profits from the slave trade ranged from 50 per cent to 100 per cent during the early eighteenth century. Bristol was already a comparatively wealthy city prior to this trade; as one of the three points of the slave triangle (the others being Africa and the West Indies), the city prospered. This triangle was called the Triangular Trade.

Blackbeard – pirate

Edward Teach (c. 1680 – 22 November 1718), better known as Blackbeard for his wild black hair (to which he attached lighted matches), was a notorious English buccaneer of the eighteenth century. He was most likely born in Bristol, and joined the crew of Benjamin Hornigold in about 1716. He quickly moved on to captain his own ship, the infamous Queen Anne's Revenge, and terrorised the High Seas between 1717 and 1718.

Traffic congestion

Everyone who lives in – and more importantly, tries to get around – Bristol knows it has a traffic problem. Many solutions have been suggested over the years, the latest ideas being congestion charging, 'showcase' bus lanes and a new tram.

Tobacco industry

Bristol, one of the UK's largest ports, was pivotal to many industries, including the tobacco trade. W.D. & H.O. Wills of Bristol was one of the founding members of Imperial Tobacco, and is still the headquarters for that group. The Wills Memorial takes its name from the George and Henry Wills of the same family, who also funded the building. It is the world's fourth largest such company.

St Paul's riot

The St Paul's riot occurred on 2 April 1980 when the Black and White Café on Grosvenor Road was raided. One hundred and thirty people were arrested, twenty-five hospitalised and several fire-engines and police cars were damaged. St Paul's at the time was notorious for the poor quality of its housing, an issue which, along with mounting racial tensions in the area, made this part of Bristol very volatile – and the raid sparked off an enormous protest against the authorities that lasted for several hours. After the riot, which drew an immense amount of media attention to the area, conditions began to improve. The Black and White Café was demolished in 2005.

Headlines and Letters

Outbreak!

'There is a considerable outbreak in Bristol of pinkeyed fever among horses.' (*The Bristol Mercury*, 1 January 1900)

Shocking death at a fire at Brislington

'Shortly after one o'clock on Tuesday morning the villagers of Brislington were aroused by an alarm of "fire", and it was found that a stable and room over it… were in flames. It was known that Harper [the tenant], who is a haulier and coal seller, kept a horse and cart in the stable and outbuildings, but on the villagers assembling round the spot it was found impossible to make any attempt to save anything within the building.' (*Bristol Mercury and Western Counties Advertiser*, 24 June 1876)

Party in a field, 1876

'Mr Joseph Lyon, of East Harptree… was summoned by the police authorities for allowing persons to take intoxicating liquors for the purpose of being drunk in a field belonging to Mr J. Stallard.' (The *Bristol Mercury and Western Counties Advertiser,* 24 June 1876)

Gardening woes

'Yate woman evicted – for messy garden.' (*Bristol Evening Post*, 2 May 2008)

Crop circles' creators caught on camera?

'It could be the first and most compelling evidence of a mysterious creator of Wiltshire's famous crop circles – a flash of white light and a crop circle appears in front of startled researchers.' (*Bristol Evening Post*, 20 July 2007)

No lights and rude

'I reprimanded two adult cyclists on pedestrian-busy Wine Street for riding on the pavement. One of them, after abuse, said he was not allowed on the road. He had no lights! Neither had the other. Both were in their 30s. On getting off a bus onto a narrow pavement in Sandy Park Road 25 minutes later I was struck by a woman cyclist riding without lights on the pavement. She accused me of not looking where I was going… Is there a cycling Mafia around in Bristol?' (*Bristol Evening Post*, 25 November 2010)

Bristol Postcards: College Green

Museums, Galleries & Attractions

SS *Great Britain*, Great Western Dockyard, Gas Ferry Road
Dedicated to the world's first great ocean liner and her famous
engineer, Brunel. Voted the UK's large visitor attraction of the year
2007. Built and launched in Bristol in 1843.

Blaise Castle House Museum and Estate, Henbury
Nineteenth-century mansion set in 400 acres of parkland with a
folly castle. The nearby Blaise hamlet of nine picturesque cottages
was designed by John Nash in 1809 to accommodate Blaise estate
pensioners.

Bristol Museum & Art Gallery, Queens Road, Clifton
Features collections of art and archaeology, geology and natural
history, housed in a magnificent Edwardian baroque building at
the top of Park Street.

The Georgian House, Great George Street
An eighteenth-century, six-storey townhouse, restored and
decorated to its original glory, making it one of the most complete
houses of its kind. It was built in 1790 for John Pinney, a wealthy
slave plantation owner and sugar merchant.

Clifton Suspension Bridge and visitor centre,
Bridge Road, Leigh Woods
Designed by the great Victorian engineer Isambard Kingdom
Brunel, although he did not live to see his creation finished in
1864. Thousands of visitors stroll across the bridge for views of
the ancient Avon Gorge, elegant Clifton and the city beyond.

Paintworks Event Space, Arnos Vale
Gallery and event space off Bath Road in Brislington hosting
regular events and exhibitions.

Arnolfini, Narrow Quay, Harbourside
Gallery, café, bar and bookshop and a leading centre for the
contemporary arts, housed in a converted warehouse situated in
the heart of the harbourside area. Features exhibitions, cinema,
performance, dance, talks and events.

Royal West of England Academy of Arts, Queens Road Clifton
Five naturally lit galleries and a commercial space too.

Kings Weston Roman Villa, Lawrence Weston
Featuring a Roman bath suite and mosaic floors. Fully excavated between 1948-50, it was discovered during the construction of Lawrence West housing estate.

M Shed, Bristol Docks
Opened in 2011 on the site of the former Industrial Museum, this comprises three main galleries featuring people and places in Bristol.

Red Lodge, Park Row
Built in 1580, it is furnished in Elizabethan, Stuart and Georgian styles and contains the impressive Great Oak Room, with its original Elizabethan plasterwork ceiling, oak panelling and carved chimneypiece.

Bristol Zoo Gardens, Guthrie Road, Clifton
Set within 12 acres of gardens with over 450 species of exotic and endangered animals from the four corners of the globe.

Bristol Blue Glass Factory and Shop, Whitby Road, St Phillips
Famous glassworks that have been synonymous with Bristol for the past four centuries.

Arnos Vale Cemetery Trust, Bath Road, Brislington
Opened in 1837, following the cholera epidemic that first struck the city in 1832. More than 300,000 people are buried or remembered on the site, including many social reformers, celebrities, religious pioneers and nautical and military heroes.

Blue Reef Aquarium & IMAX 3D cinema, Anchor Road, Harbourside
This aquarium transports visitors to the spectacular 'underwater gardens' of the Mediterranean and stunning beauty of tropical waters – home to everything from seahorses and puffer fish to tropical sharks. There is a coral reef housed within a gigantic ocean display, home to exotic species of fish. There's also a programme of free daily events including entertaining talks and feeding displays as well as the IMAX cinema that will take you on a 3D journey.

Watershed Media Centre, Canon's Road, Harbourside

Alongside Bristol Docks, the Watershed is not just a very popular meeting place with its café/bar, but houses a number of cinemas and galleries. It runs a constantly changing programme of films, events, talks and exhibitions.

@ Bristol, Anchor Road, Harbourside

@Bristol is a registered charity and one of the UK's leading science and discovery centres, where exploration and education go hand-in-hand.

Tobacco Factory, Southville

Theatre, live music, café and bar, dance studio, room hire and events. It acts as a meeting point for the community and now has a Sunday market with a strong bias towards ethical, eco-friendly, fair trade, organic and local products.

Buildings

Timber-framed houses
Llandoger Trow, King Street – seventeenth century.
Shakespeare Inn, Temple Street – more or less unchanged since 1636.
St Michael's Hill – various.

Almshouses
Foster's Almshouses, Colston Street – originally founded by a bequest from fifteenth-century merchant John Foster. The wings of the current building were built between 1861 and 1883.
John Barstaple Almshouse, Old Market Street – originally built in 1395 but has had to be rebuilt over the years and the present building dates back to mid-Victorian times. Founded by the former sheriff and three times mayor of Bristol, John Barstaple.
Lady Haberfield's Almshouse, Joy Hill off Hotwell Road – built in 1891.
Merchant Venturers Almshouses, King Street – built in 1696 for elderly and convalescent sailors.

Georgian
Coopers Hall façade, Theatre Royal, King Street – incorporated into what is now the Old Vic theatre complex in the 1970s. Designed by William Halfpenny in the 1740s with a Corinthian portico and large windows.
Corn Exchange, Corn Street – 1743.
Queen Square
Hotwells
Royal Fort House, Clifton
Royal York Crescent, Clifton – began building in 1791, completed 1820.
Sion Hill, Clifton
Berkley Square

Victorian

Temple Meads – opened in August 1840, designed by Brunel, grade II listed building.

Great Western Hotel – now Brunel House (Council Offices), 1830s.

Guildhall – Gothic Revival designed by R.S. Pope, 1843.

Assize Courts – designed by T.S. Pope, late 1860s.

No. 55 Corn Street – Venetian influence based on St Mark's Library, 1850s.

Lower Hirst, close to Sea Walls on the Downs – 1860.

Bristol Byzantine

(deep red Cattybrook bricks made in Almondsbury)

Granary, Welsh Back – designed by Archibald Ponston and William Venn Gough, 1869.

Fishmarket, Baldwin Street

Victoria Street

Old Tramways Generating Station – later part of Courage's Brewer

Arts & Crafts

Edward Everard printing works, Broad Street – 1900.

1960s and '70s buildings

Templar House

Robinson Building – 1966, 200ft tall.

Tollgate House – sixteen storeys high, recently demolished for Cabot Circus development.

Lloyd's Building, Canons' Marsh

Bristol and West tower – seventeen storeys, now redeveloped.

Since 2000

Explore @ Bristol – Imax cinema and the 'perched butterfly' roof shape of the Blue Reef Aquarium.

Imaginarium – silver ball reflecting the continual activity in the public square.

Cabot Circus shopping centre

Developments in Floating Harbour

Capricorn Quay, Hotwell Road

The Point, Wapping Wharf

Colston Hall foyer – replaced the former gas showroom building of 1935.

Some Notable Buildings

St Nicholas covered market (old)
Built in 1743, this picturesque market at the top of Corn Street was voted one of the best markets in the UK by the *Guardian* in 2010.

Wills Tower (gaudy)
This Gothic building, at the top of Park Street, was built in 1915 as a memorial to Henry Overton Wills III, of tobacco company fame. At 68m tall, it can be seen from all over the city. It is one of the last great Gothic structures to be built in England.

University library (ugly and modern)
A concrete modern construction, this building is one of the least attractive of the University's properties.

Victoria Rooms (beautiful)
Built between 1838 and 1842 in a Greek revival style, this building was named in honour of Queen Victoria. It houses the University of Bristol's Music Department, and a large auditorium.

Clifton Lido (elaborate and unusual)
Hidden away on Oakfield Place in Clifton, this subscription bath was built in Egyptian style in 1849/50. In around 1990 it allegedly sprunk a leak, and didn't reopen again until 2008. Now a spa with restuarants and bars.

Llandoger Trow (very old)
A historic pub, dating from 1664, in King Street, close to the city-centre docks. A 'trow' is a flat-bottomed barge, and these barges traditionally sailed to trade in Bristol.

Spectrum (ugly and '80s)
At the foot of the M32, this is one of the more prominent, glass-clad office buildings as you enter the city.

Cabot Circus (eye-catching)
Costing £500 million to build, this is an elegant and eye-catching addition to the cityscape. Encompasses the old Dominican friary buildings.

Buildings: Front and Back

Buildings: Outside and Inside

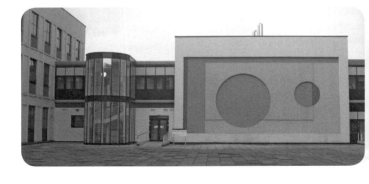

Bristol Postcards:
River Avon from Clifton Downs

Flora and Fauna

Bristol has three rare plants named after it:

Bristol Onion (*Allium Sphaerocephalon*): also known as a round-headed leek, it has purple-red flowers and grows to approximately 30cm high.

Bristol Rockcress (*Arabis scabra*): each plant has just a few creamy-white flowers, surrounded by very dark green leaves.

Bristol Whitebeam (*Sorbus bristoliensis*): a species of tree that can be found widely across the UK, but the Bristol species differs in that it has slightly different leaves, which are a shade of green rather than white on the underside.

Also to be found in Bristol:

Wild service tree (*Sorbus torminalis*): a broadleaf tree with leaves similar to a maple.

Western spiked speedwell (*Veronica spicata*): tall, candle-like flowers that can be shades of blue, white or red.

Red and fallow deer: found in the deer park at Ashton Court estate.

Swans: large flocks can be seen living within Bristol city docks. They owe their continued existence to the endeavours of a group known as the Friends of Bristol Swans, a registered charity.

Parks, Green Spaces, Allotments and City Farms

The Downs: Clifton Down and Durdham Down cover about 400 acres. Popular for sport, picnics and wildlife spotting.

Ashton Court: The home of many of the city's festivals and events, the grounds of the mansion house offer access to 850 acres of woodland and meadows.

Brandon Hill: One of the oldest parks in the UK. It came into the possession of the Bristol Corporation in 1174, was sublet to farmers until 1625 and has been open to the public ever since. Its position, half way up Park Street, makes it an excellent spot for panoramic views over the city.

Castle Park: Situated by the riverside and housing the remains of a great medieval castle, this is a central green space.

College Green: At around 3 acres, this open space by the cathedral is a favourite spot for lunchtime picnics.

Eastville Park: A grand Victorian city park, well known for its lake.

Snuff Mills, Stapleton: A tranquil area in Stapleton, North Bristol, this park contains an old quarry and a stone mill. The steep wooded banks of the River Frome are popular for strolling along and spotting otters.

St Andrew's Park: Laid out in 1895, this Victorian pleasure ground has children's play areas and tea rooms.

Badock's Wood Nature Reserve: Named after prominent local industrialist Sir Stanley Hugh Badock, born in Bristol in 1867.

Blaise Castle and Hamlet: an eighteenth-century mansion and grounds in Henbury, with 650 acres of grounds open to the public. The 'castle' refers to a folly above the gorge rather than the mansion itself.

Bristol to Bath cycle path: a 13 mile railway path connecting the two cities.

Windmill Hill City Farm: Formed in 1976 by a group of local volunteers, there are farmyard animals to see, gardens to explore and environmental and craft courses to sample.

St Werburgh's City Farm: Suitably situated on Watercress Road, watercress beds once covered the site until a street of terraced houses was built in 1910. In the 1970s, the street became derelict and the houses were pulled down, making way for a group of volunteers to set up the farm in 1980.

104 Allotment Sites: These are situated all over the city and are always in demand for residents to grow their own fruit and vegetables. Due to the diversity of plants grown on these allotments, they are havens for many types of wildlife.

Home-Grown Companies

BAE Systems, Filton
British Aerospace Electronic Systems is a global company employing approximately 100,000 people worldwide. They provide products and services for air, land and naval forces as well as electronics, security information, technology solutions and support services. The history of the company can be traced back to 1560.

Airbus, Filton
A leading aircraft manufacturer, recently involved in the creation of wings for the new Airbus A380.

Hewlett-Packard, Filton
The Bristol site of this computer company is the second largest central research location for the business. The University of the West of England is now offering a degree in Enterprise Computing with the company.

Rolls-Royce, Patchway
The Bristol branch has been responsible for aero-engine manufacturing since 1910. Important historical collections are housed at the Bristol site, within the military aero-engine facility, and can be viewed by appointment.

MoD, Filton
The purpose-built Abbey Wood complex was opened in 1995 and is home to the Procurement Executive. Its employees have their own railway station.

Cameron Balloons, Bedminster
Established in 1971, this is the world's largest manufacturer of hot-air balloons.

Imperial Tobacco
A global tobacco company with headquarters in Bristol, Imperial Tobacco is the fourth largest tobacco company in the world.

Largest Employers

Company Name	No. of Employees	Sector
Bristol City Council	16,000	Government Services
Ministry of Defence	7,000	Government Services
Bristol NHS Foundation Trust	6,000	Heathcare & Welfare services
Lloyds TSB Group	6,000	Financial Services
University of Bristol	5,000	Education
Airbus	5,000	Manufacturing
Rolls-Royce	3,500	Manufacturing
AXA Life	2,000	Financial Services
Avon & Somerset Police	1,000 to 2,500	Public Protection Services
Avon Fire & Rescue Service	1,000 to 2,500	Public Protection Services
Network Rail	1,000 to 2,500	Transport Services
Royal Mail	1,000 to 2,500	Distribution
DHL Supply Chain	700 to 1,000	Distribution
RAC Motoring Services	500 to 700	Transport Services

(Source: www.investinbristol.com)

Job Sectors

Jobs by industry

Manufacturing	13,200	5.7 per cent
Construction	8,200	3.5 per cent
Distribution, hotels & restaurants	46,500	20.1 per cent
Transport & communications	9,900	4.3 per cent
Finance, IT & other business activities	76,500	33 per cent
Public admin, education & health	66,600	28.7 per cent
Other services	9,700	4.2 per cent
Of these, tourism related	14,500	6.3 per cent

Employment by occupation

Managers & senior officials	27,300	12.6 per cent
Professional occupations	42,400	19.6 per cent
Associate professional & technical	38,600	17.9 per cent
Administrative & secretarial	20,400	9.4 per cent
Skilled trades and occupations	15,500	7.2 per cent
Personal service occupations	17,100	7.9 per cent
Sales & customer service occupations	15,400	7.2 per cent
Process plant & machinery occupations	14,900	6.9 per cent
Elementary occupations	23,900	11.1 per cent

Total number of employees	231,600	
Full-time	156,700	67.7 per cent
Part-time	74,800	32.3 per cent

(Source: ONS annual business inquiry employee analysis July 2009-June 2010)

Born in Bristol

Allen Lane	21/9/1902	Formed Penguin Books in 1935
Archibald Sayce	25/9/1846	Philologist
Banksy	1974	Graffiti artist
Cary Grant	18/1/1904	Film actor
Chris Morris	15/6/1962	Actor, comedy writer & satirist
Christopher Fry	18/12/1907	Dramatist
Damien Hurst	7/6/1965	Painter & installation artist
Edward Godwin	6/10/1886	Architect & designer
Edward Tyson	1650	Physician
Hugh Conway	26/12/1847	Novelist
Issac Rosenberg	25/11/1890	Poet & artist
J.K. Rowling	31/7/1965	Author of the Harry Potter series of books
John Gully	21/8/1783	Sportsman - boxing champion and horse racing
John Symonds	5/10/1840	Writer
Johnny Ball	28/5/1938	TV personality
Julie Burchill	3/7/1959	Novelist and journalist
Mary Robinson	27/11/1757	Actress, poet and novelist
Michael Redgrave	20/3/1908	Film and stage actor
Percy Nunn	1870	Education administrator
Richard Bright	28/9/1789	Physician
Richard Long	2/6/1945	Land artist
Robert Southey	12/8/1774	Poet
Robin Cousins	17/8/1957	Figure skater
Rosemary Butcher	1947	Choreographer
Samuel Plimsoll	10/2/1824	Social reformer

Thomas Chatterton	20/11/1752	Poet
Thomas Lawrence	13/4/1769	Painter
Thomas Longman	1699	Publisher
Thomas Lovell Beddoes	30/6/1803	Physiologist and writer
W.G. Grace	18/7/1848	Cricketer
William Combe	1741	Satirist
William Rees-Mogg	14/7/1928	Journalist
William Slim	6/8/1891	Soldier

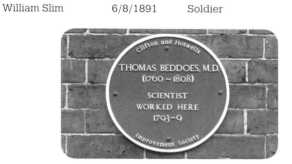

Died in Bristol

Thomas Longman	1755	Family originally Bristol soapboilers. Founded publishing company Longmans & Co.
John Breillat	1856	Formed the Bristol Coal Gas Co.
Philip George	1828	Started Georges Brewery business – boasted some of the largest vats in the world holding 1,300 barrels. He was three times sheriff of Bristol.
Edward Hodges Baily	1867	Bristol-born sculptor best known for the Nelson on Nelson's Column.
Ernest Bevin	1951	Member of Churchill's Cabinet and Foreign Secretary from 1945 to 1951.
Elizabeth Blackwell	1821	First woman doctor.
Matthew Brickdale	1831	MP for Bristol in 1788 who seconded the motion to reject the Slavery Regulation Bill, which paved the way for the abolition of slavery.
Captain Woodes Rogers	1732	In his voyage around the world, he stopped at the island of Juan Fernandez in 1709 and discovered Alexander Selkirk, who had been shipwrecked and living on the island for nearly four and a half years.
Edward Teach	1718	Known as 'Blackbeard'.
Jane Jackson Roeckel	1907	Pianist and composer under pseudonym Jules de Sevrai.
Edward Colston	1721	Philanthropist and son of William Colston. Founded Colston School.

Raja Rammohun Roy	1833	Indian religious, social and educational reformer who challenged traditional Hindu culture and indicated the lines of progress for Indian society under British rule. Buried at Arnos Vale cemetery.
Richard Reynolds	1816	Philanthropist and founded the Samaritans.
Matthew Wasborough	1781	Inventor of the flywheel.
John L. McAdam	1836	Inventor of the tarmac road surface.

Blue Plaques

John James, CBE (1906-1996). Philanthropist, 96 Philip Street, Bedminster (site of the Windmill Hill City Farm).

Eric Ball, OBE (1903-1989). Salvationist and composer, Salvation Army Hall, Two Mile Hill Road.

Bob Hope (1903-2003). Comedian and entertainer, St George's Park, St George, Church Road entrance.

Nipper the Dog (1884-1895), 'His Masters Voice'. Corner of Park Row/Woodland Road. Mark Barraud, owner and master of Bristol-born dog Nipper, was employed as a scenic director in the old Prince's Theatre in Park Row.

Michael Redgrave (1908-1982). Actor, 4 Horfield Road, off St Michaels Hill.

Sir Robert Stephens (1931-1995). Early star of the National Theatre, London stage and screen actor, 34 Priory Road, Shirehampton – lived here from 1931-1939.

Henry Wills (1856-1922). Engineer and Philanthropist, 23 Blenheim Road, off Coldharbour Road, Redland.

Russ Conway (1925-2000). Pianist, composer & entertainer, 2 Dean Lane, Southville.

Mary Carpenter (1807-1877). Educational and social reformer, buried in Arnos Vale cemetery, Red Lodge, Park Row.

Hannah More (1745-1833). Educational pioneer, Keeper's Cottage, Brislington Hill.

Norah Cooke-Hurle (1871-1960). Educationalist and pioneer in mental health, Stars & Stripes Pool Hall, Brislington Hill.

Hannah More
1745 - 1833

Educator, writer and
social reformer, started
the first school in
Brislington at Keepers
Cottage c1796

**Norah Cooke - Hurle
(born Fry)**
1871 - 1960

Educationalist and Mental
Health Pioneer lived at
Brislington Hill House
on this site from
1915 - 1921

MARY CARPENTER
LADY BYRON
REFORMATORY
1854

Interesting People Associated with Bristol

John Loudon McAdam, 1756-1836

A Scot, McAdam moved to Bristol in 1812. His technique of 'macadamising' roads revolutionalised travel.

Woodes Rogers, 1679-1732

An English sea captain and privateer, later the first Royal Governor of the Bahamas. He is known as the captain of the vessel that rescued the marooned Alexander Selkirk, whose plight is believed to have inspired Daniel Defoe's Robinson Crusoe. He died in Bristol.

James Hillier Blount, aka James Blunt, 1974-

He attended Bristol University before becoming an officer in the Life Guards, British Army. He has gone on to be an extremely successful singer-songwriter and musician, winning two BRIT Awards, two Ivor Novello Awards and being nominated for five Grammy Awards.

Paul Boateng, 1951-

Born in London, he read law at the University of Bristol and became the UK's first black Cabinet Minister in 2002 when he was appointed as Chief Secretary to the Treasury. He is now a member of the House of Lords.

Hugh Cornwell, 1949-

Famous for the band The Stranglers, he studied biochemistry at Bristol University.

Archibald Alexander Leach, known as Cary Grant, 1904-1986

Born in Horfield, he was expelled from Fairfield Grammar School in 1918. He joined the Bob Pender stage troupe, where he performed as a stilt walker, and travelled to America in 1920 on a two-year tour. He stayed in the US, and his success in Hollywood began in 1931. Thereafter he was nominated for two Academy Awards in the 1940s, and received a special Academy Award for Lifetime Achievement in 1970. In 1981 he was accorded the Kennedy Center Honors.

Criminals

1820: Hannah Ainsworth was charged with receiving stolen goods and sentenced to fourteen years' transportation.

1823: William Cartney (a bankrupt) was charged with fraudulently and feloniously embezzling part of his effects and sentenced to transportation for life.

1827: William Barrett was charged with robbery in a counting house and sentenced to transportation for life.

1828: William Badgett was charged with highway robbery and sentenced to death.

First hanging at Bristol Gaol – in 1821, eighteen-year old John Horwood was convicted of the murder of a girl he was infatuated with – he hit her on the head with a large stone.

Last hanging at Bristol Gaol – in 1849, Sarah Harriet Thomas was convicted of the murder of her elderly employer, who was found beaten to death in her own bed.

Making a monkey of the law: Bristol University students Fred Hooper and Ron Morgan stole a 7ft tall stuffed gorilla called Alfred from Bristol City Museum during rag week in 1956, which sparked a police investigation.

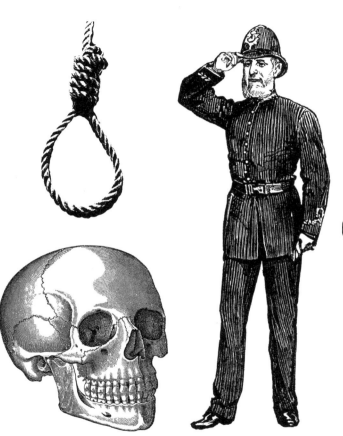

Ghosts

Llandoger Trow, King Street – alleged to have fifteen ghosts. The most popular ghost is the young child said to haunt the top floor. Footsteps are heard on the stairs at night.

All Saints' Church – a Black Monk is believed to return to watch over a pile of treasure which he had hidden during his lifetime.

Arnos Manor Hotel, Room 160 – a pregnant nun took her own life, and her sisters bricked her body up in an alcove.

Ashton Court Estate – decapitated horseman. Also reports of 'Grey Ladies' and a phantom hound.

BBC Bristol, Whiteladies Road – poltergeist, said to be responsible for many electrical breakdowns.

Clifton Suspension Bridge – the shades seen drifting around on the bridge are said to belong to those who have jumped off, taking their own lives.

Fire Brigade Headquarters, Temple Back – the Knights Templar once owned lands around Bristol, and this one appears in medieval dress.

King William III pub, King Street – staff have claimed to hear their names being called out, even when they are alone in the pub.

Old Vic Theatre, King Street – Sarah Siddons' boyfriend hanged himself in the theatre and her ghost, wearing a white crinoline dress, is thought to continue to mourn the loss.

Parry's Lane, The Downs – the lane takes its name from a well which once stood in the area, a well where a man named Parry slit his own throat. His ghost is said to remain in the area.

SS Great Britain – reports of sightings of a ghostly, middle-aged man. He allegedly matches the description of Captain John Gray, who vanished in 1872.

I Love Bristol Because…

…it's a city AND a county.

…the rock slide by the suspension bridge is brilliant to play on.

…of its hills, which give amazing views from various angles at the same time as being a short walk to the city centre.

…Gloucester Road is full of fantastic independent shops.

…the architecture is beautiful and varied, with tall Georgian townhouses, high garden walls and quiet cobbled streets.

…there are so many hidden pubs to discover – the Green Man and the Hare on the Hill in Kingsdown, to name just two.

…you can take a little local train line from Temple Meads to Severn Beach.

…it's only a short drive to the holiday destinations of Devon and Cornwall.

…it's small enough to walk around easily and bump into friends frequently, at the same time as being sufficiently large to have excellent shops and nightlife.

…Bedminster has some of the best charity shops.

I Hate Bristol Because...

...bikes (or parts of bikes) are frequently stolen.

...in term time there are hordes of students in the Clifton and Redland areas.

...it is difficult to park a car if you live in the city centre.

...the level of traffic congestion is extremely bad – it is one of the most congested 'core' cities outside London.

...public transport is expensive and unreliable.

...Corn Street, between midnight and 3 a.m. over the weekend, is full of drunk people.

...there always seems to be a steep hill to climb to get from A to B.

Favourite Scene

The Docks are a focal point in the city and the views by night or day, from one of the many hills or from a central tall building, are truly spectacular and never cease to amaze, however familiar you become with the city.

Least Favourite Scene

Traffic jams on the M32, particularly after a long journey home, departing the M4, whizzing along the M32 until close to the city – and then being gridlocked for the last few yards.

SS *Great Britain*

When launched in 1843, the SS *Great Britain* was by far the largest vessel afloat. However, her protracted construction and high cost had left her owners in a difficult financial position, and they were forced out of business in 1846 after the ship was stranded by a navigational error. Sold for salvage and repaired, she carried thousands of immigrants to Australia until converted to sail in 1881. Three years later, the vessel was retired to the Falkland Islands, where she was used as a warehouse, quarantine ship and coal hulk.

The SS *Great Britain* finally returned to Bristol after 8,000 miles at sea in 1970. The rusting iron hulk of the ship was rescued from lying abandoned in the Falkland Islands. A huge crowd welcomed her home as she was towed under the Clifton Suspension Bridge and back into the dock.

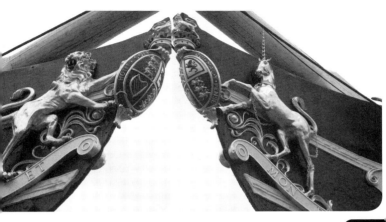

Bristol Postcards:
St Augustine's Bridge

Bristol Postcards: Suspension Bridge from the Cliffs

Local Lingo

Terminal L – an L sound is appended to words that end in a letter A (i.e. area becomes 'areal' and Ikea 'Ikeal'.

Dialect known colloquially as Brizzle or Bristle – rhotic dialect in which the R in words like car is pronounced.

Gert lush – really good.

Cod lot – fish and chips.

Hark at ee – listen to him.

Where's that to? – where is it?

I was led down – I was lying down.

They's – They are.

Mind – You know what I mean.

My lover – mate/pal.

He can do it hisself – he can do it himself.

Babba – baby.

Daps – plimsolls, trainers.

Customs and Traditions

Bristol nails: outside the eighteenth-century Exchange Buildings in Corn Street stand the four bronze, flat-topped Bristol nails. They date from the sixteenth century, and historically merchants placed their money on the nails to seal a deal, hence the expression 'to pay on the nail'.

February – Rag Week (rag standing for raising and giving). This is held in university towns across the country, including Bristol, to raise money for charity. Students undertake all sorts of madcap activities and parade through the city asking for donations.

May Day – merry-making and maypole dancing.

May – Jack-in-the-Green: the symbol of the beginning of summer, he and his followers dance and play music whilst parading around the city.

July – Canynges Society. In remembrance of William Canynges the Younger (1402-1474), a fifteenth-century merchant who invested much of his wealth into restoring St Mary Redcliffe church. The Society remember him every year.

July – St Paul's Carnival, held since 1967: began as a celebration of black and Irish culture in the St Paul's area of Bristol. The carnival is awash with amazing homemade costumes, floats, music and dancing

July – graduation ceremony for Bristol University students, centered around the Wills Memorial building at the top of Park Street.

September – Open Doors' Day: a chance to see inside various important historic buildings around Bristol that are not usually open to the public.

September – Raja Rammohun Roy: every year visitors from the Indian sub-Continent visit the shrine to this education and social reformer, who is buried in Arnos Vale cemetery.

105

Festivals

Bristol International Balloon Fiesta – August, Ashton Court. Began in 1978.

Bristol International Festival of Kites and Air Creations – September, Ashton Court. Began in 1986.

St Paul's Carnival – July, St Paul's. Began in 1967.

Bristol Harbour Festival – July/August, The Docks. Began in 1971.

Slapstick Silent Comedy Festival – January, various venues. Began in 2005.

Encounters International Short Film Festival – November, Watershed. Began in 1995.

Wildscreen Film Festival – October, Watershed.Began in 1986 (held every other year).

Bristol Bike Fest – June, Ashton Court. Began in 2008.

Bristol Children's Festival – August, The Downs.

Soil Association Organic Food Festival – September, Harbourside. Began in 2001.

Bristol International Animation Festival – April, Watershed. Began in 2000.

Secret Bristol

Birdcage Walk, Clifton – a peaceful path through a well-kept graveyard in the centre of Clifton, particularly beautiful with the plants and arbours in the spring and summer.

Coronation Tap, Clifton – one of Bristol's many well-hidden tiny pubs.

Giant's Ghyston's Cave – 250ft above the valley floor, close to the Clifton Suspension Bridge for a view from a very unusual angle. Incredible view of the Avon Gorge, accessed via a narrow tunnel through the rocks.

Avery's Wine Cellar – now found in Culver Street, just a short distance from the original premises on Park Street. The cellars feature incredible vaulted ceilings that once housed the bottling line and blending tanks.

La Rocca nightclub – a downstairs cavern of a club on Clifton Triangle, very popular with students.

Clifton Lido – once a Victorian lido, it has now been refurbished after years of standing derelict into a spa and restaurant.

Casamia – Michelin star Italian restaurant, Westbury-on-Trym.

St George's, Brandon Hill – concert hall and recording studios known for its fine acoustics.

Cube Microplex Cinema, Dove Street South, Kings Square, Kingsdown – 'social' cinemas, cocktails and ice cream with your film, live music to accompany movies, music with visuals, talks. Once shared its entrance with The Chinese Overseas Association and Mayflower Chinese restaurant, now a micro disco bar.

Folk House – adult education centre hidden away down an alley off Park Street.

Spike Island – area adjoining the city centre. Comprises a strip of land between the Floating Harbour to the north and the tidal new cut of the River Avon to the south, from the dock entrance to the west to Bathurst Basin in the east. Bristol Harbour Railway runs the length of the island and used to connect the working areas with the railway network. No longer a true 'island'. Spike Island Artspace is situated in the former tea-packing factory.

Clifton Rocks railway – lower terminus in Hotwells is now bricked up. Opened in 1893. Brick tunnel in the steep cliff was 450ft long, 27ft wide and 17ft high, and the tracks were at a gradient of more than one in two. The journey took forty seconds.

Christmas Steps – the steep-slanted steps were constructed in September 1669 and were paid for by a wealthy wine merchant. The steps are grade II listed, and are a maze of arched alleyways and secret passages full of artisan shops and galleries.

Best Graffiti

Banksy – various locations.

'No Tesco' graffiti stencils up and down Gloucester Road – Tesco want to move into the site of former Jesters Comedy Club on Cheltenham Road.

Clockwork Orange & Blue Mountain clubs.

Herbert's Bakery, Montpelier – various characters alongside a menu of breads on offer.

'Bling' camel with built-in stereo – St Paul's.

Local Sports Teams

Bristol City Football Club, founded in 1894
Mascot – Scrumpy the Robin.
Nickname – the Robins.
Anthems – Wurzels 'One for Bristol City'; Bounce .
around the Ground.
Famous fans – Jonathan Pearce, Tony Robinson,
Marcus Trescothick.

Bristol Rovers Football Club, founded in 1883
Mascot – Captain Black Arab.
Nicknames – Pirates (official), Gasheads (unofficial).
Famous fans – Jeffrey Archer.
Song – Rod Hull, 'Bristol Rovers All the Way'; Goodnight Irene.

Bristol Rugby, founded in 1888
Mascot – Brizzley Bear.
Nickname – Shoguns, temporarily, from 2001 to 2005,
due to a sponsorship deal with Mitsubishi.

Gloucestershire County Cricket Club
Home ground in Bristol.

Bristol Pirates Basketball Club
Knowle.

Bristol Aztecs American Football team
Filton.

Bristol Pitbulls – ice hockey, founded in 2009
Based at the John Nike Ice Rink in Frogmore Street.

Sports Teams: Facts and Figures

Bristol City Football Club

Founded when Bristol South End turned professional. Merged with Bedminster in 1900, joined the Football League in 1901, and beat Blackpool in their first ever game 2-0. They play at Ashton Gate.

Bristol Rovers Football Club

Founded as the 'Black Arabs'. They were Eastville Rovers, then Bristol Eastville Rovers before they took their current name in 1898. Members of the football league since 1920. Now play at the Memorial Stadium.

Bristol Rugby

Formerly known as Bristol Football Club.
Great names include Len Corbett, Sam Tucker, Jack Gregory, John Pullin, Alan Morley, Jason Little and Agustin Pichot. Home ground – the Memorial Ground from 1921, dedicated as a memorial to local rugby players who fell in the First World War. The very first match played in 1888 was a heavy away defeat against Cardiff. Under the captaincy of Tommy Thomson in 1891/92, Bristol won twenty games out of twenty-four. 1971/72 was the club's best ever season, with 1,000 points scored for the first time. The 2001/02 season saw the corporate boxes sell out for the first time.

Gloucestershire County Cricket Club

W.G. Grace played for this side. They hosted the first British Indoor Cricket World Cup, and they play at the Imperial Tobacco ground.

Bristol Storm Basketball Club

Play at the Filton College WISE campus.

Bristol Badgers Baseball

American sports thrive in the city. Baseball in Bristol has its home at Southmead Community Sports Centre.

Bristol Aztecs American Football Team

This premier division team has two rival teams from each of the universities. The Barracudas play for Bristol, and the Bullets play for UWE.

Australian Rules Football

Sport from even further afield: Australian rules football has been played in Bristol since 1990, and is still going strong. The 'Dockers' have links with Western Gaels Gaelic Football Club, who are based in Bristol, with a lot of players turning out for both sides.

Bristol Handball Club

Just the one handball club in the city, at the Academy and the Princess Royal Sports complex in Somerset. The game is mainly played in Europe.

Downs Football League

Durdham Downs are used each week by the Downs Football League with numerous pitches marked out.

A-Z

A Artistic – so many local artists and events to enjoy.

B Bristle/Brizzle – dialect.

C Clifton Suspension Bridge.

D Docks – central hub of the city.

E *Exit Through the Gift Shop* – the name of a film made by Bristol graffiti artist Banksy which was nominated for an Oscar in 2011.

F Fireboat – Pyronaut built in 1934.

G Grotto – shell-lined grotto at Goldney House, Clifton. Not open to the public but worth a look if you get to go to an event there.

H Horfield – was considered by travellers to be a lawless place in olden times due to the fact that the nearby extensive Horfield Wood was the haunt of vagrants and criminals.

I Inns – Bristol is awash with historic pubs.

J Jacob's Wells Road, Hotwells – home to the Avon Wildlife Trust, Bristol Community Dance Centre and the Hope & Anchor pub. Jacob's Well refers to Britain's only known medieval Jewish ritual bath.

K Kitchen – Bike Kitchens are run all over Bristol and provide access to professional tools and advice from experienced bike mechanics for free.

L Largest city in the south west of England.

M Music – known for its rich musical talent such as Massive Attack & Portishead.

N Normans – Bristol Castle was built by the Normans and was demolished in 1650 by Act of Parliament.

O Oldest surviving steam tug in the world – built in 1861, the *Mayflower* is moored in the Docks.

P Pero's Footbridge – constructed in 1999, it links the harbourside areas.

Q QEH Theatre – a modern building which is part of Queen Elizabeth's Hospital school in Clifton.

R River Avon – a bridge was built across the river to create the original settlement of Bristol.

S Steam crane – Fairbairn Steam Crane built in 1878 and was in regular use until 1973 loading and unloading ships and railway wagons.

T Tobacco Factory – theatre and bar in Southville.

U University Precinct – area in the city centre populated with numerous University of Bristol buildings.

V Viaduct – Cheltenham Road Viaduct, known as The Arches, was built in 1874 to link Montpelier and Redland railway stations.

W Wills Memorial Building – commissioned by the magnates of the Bristol tobacco company W D & H O Wills. Landmark building of the University of Bristol at the top of Park Street.

X Xylophone – five xylophone teachers live in Bristol alone.

Y Young Bristol – Bristol's largest youth work charity works with young people across the Greater Bristol area running projects that build young people's confidence, give them new practical skills and a sense of purpose and self-worth.

Z Zoo, established in 1836.

Websites

www.visit.bristol.co.uk – visitor information.

www.about-bristol.co.uk – picture tours and history of Bristol.

www.electricpavilion.org – seven secret wonders of Bristol with an illustrated map.

www.gurtlushonline.co.uk – stories and archive photographs from the past 100 years.

www.southmead.net – Southmead community website promoting the Cod Almighty – North Bristol's number one chip shop as voted for in a GWR competition.

www.transistionbristol.net – seeking to reduce dependence on fossil fuels and promote sustainability.

www.thisisbristol.co.uk – local online news and classifieds as well as information on what to do – restaurants, clubs, exhibitions, events.

Bristol Castle: Then and Now

Past, Present, Future

Many of Bristol's buildings have been repurposed for a new life. For example, as in many cities across the UK, Bristol's waterside is lined with old warehouse buildings, the majority of which have, over time, been converted into apartments, bringing them back to life. They include:

Robinsons Warehouse, Bathurst Parade – a grade II listed building on the Floating Harbour. It was built in 1874 by William Bruce Gingell, and used to belong to Robinson's Oil & Seed Manufactory.

Victorian warehouses, Welsh Back – Victorian waterside buildings overlook Welsh Back and have been converted into private flats. They can be seen from Redcliffe Bridge.

The Granary, Welsh Back – built in 1869 with red 'Cattybrook' brick, with black and white brick and limestone dressing – otherwise known as the Bristol Byzantine style. This former granary has been, by turns, a nightclub, a jazz club (opened by Acker Bilk himself) and a rock club. It is now apartments, with restaurants underneath.

What they thought it would look like now:

Ideas to solve Bristol's traffic congestion, the city's main problem, are legion. They include:

Mono rail – this has been discussed for many years.

Tramway – proposed to run from a car park beside the M5 at Almondsbury, through Bradley Stoke before joining existing rail tracks leading to Temple Meads. There used to be trams running along Bristol docks but these no longer run.

Future Plans

'Work has started at three sites in Bristol that brings another major new Cycling City cycle route to near completion. Once completed, The Frome Greenway will provide cyclists and pedestrians – commuters or leisure seekers alike – a largely traffic-free route from Bristol city centre, Castle Park and Cabot Circus through to UWE, MoD, AXA and beyond via Easton, Eastville and Stoke Park. Work is due to start in 2011.'
(Data from Bristol City Council website)

'Plans to sell off 90 acres of parkland will be delayed because the recession has seen land values plummet… When the plan was agreed in February last year, the council said the sale of 'marginal, surplus land' would raise cash for improvements to remaining open spaces and to create 70 new play areas over the next 20 years. A decision on which patches of Bristol City Council's 3,700 acres of parkland should go could be made during 2011.'
(*Bristol Evening Post*)

Bristol Royal Infirmary is looking into the possibility of building an air ambulance-landing facility on the roof of Queens Building – planning is yet to be approved.

M Shed is an exciting and innovative new museum for Bristol that tells the story of the city. The 1950s transit shed, originally called M Shed, on Bristol's historic wharf has been transformed into the new museum.

There are plans being developed for a new 30,000-seat stadium for Bristol City Football Club and associated development including housing, restaurants/bars, and a hotel on land at Ashton Vale and the former Alderman Moore's allotment site.

Southmead Hospital is undergoing a major change which will replace the existing Southmead and Frenchay acute hospitals. The redevelopment is due to cost around £430 million and plans to open to its first patients in 2014.

Things To Do in Bristol Checklist

Experience the view from the top of Cabot Tower

Sit on the balcony at Mud Dock on a summer evening overlooking the docks and do some people-watching

Cruise around the harbour on the *Matthew*, a modern recreation of the square rigged caravel in which John Cabot sailed from Bristol to Newfoundland in 1497

Visit Cabot Circus, Bristol's newest shopping centre, for retail therapy and interesting architecture

Take a wander around Ashton Court, with its 850 acres of woods and grasslands, deer park, two eighteen-hole pitch and putt golf courses, orienteering and mountain biking

Ride on the ferry around the harbour for a different view of Bristol from the water

Join a Pirate Walk around the city

Get yourself scared on the Haunted and Hidden Bristol Walking Tour

Visit the historic SS Great Britain – walk or take the ferry from the city centre for a tour around Brunel's historic ship

Wander around the City Museum & Art Gallery – free entry to explore the history of Bristol with special events and exhibits

Explore Arnos Vale Cemetery – historic cemetery featuring 45 acres of landscape with a diverse range of wildlife and home to graves of many celebrities, pioneers and heroes

If you were to leave Bristol by the Clifton Suspension Bridge, one of the more picturesque exits from the city, this is where you would need to have your toll money at the ready.

Picture credits

All licensed, unless stated otherwise, through Wikimedia Commons. Many thanks to all the photographers whose photographs I have used here.

Page

7. Bristol Suspension Bridge (StockXchange, uploaded by pkavitha1)

9. Bristol map (OS, 1946)

11. Map of Bristol in 1671 (*Bristol Past & Present*)

17. Jerusalem (Gugganij); Vatican City (Greudin); Hong Kong (Dice)

19. Queen Victoria (Green Lane); Neptune (Rob Brewer)

21. Tbilisi (Dmitry Gerasimov); Shangxiajiu Square, Guangzhou (ShaMianRen)

23. Bristol, Virginia (Aplomado); Newfoundland Lake, New Hampshire (Adam Backstrom); Bristol Harbour, Rhode Island (Angus Davis)

24. Abolitionist pamphlet (Library of Congress, Prints & Photographs Division, LC-USZ62-44265); The *Matthew* (Mike Peel, www.mikepeel.net)

25. SS *Great Britain* (Par Antoine)

26. Bristol Cathedral in the mid-Victorian era. (*Bristol Past & Present*)

27. Bristol Cathedral and College Green (Klafubra)

29. Castle Park in the snow (Steinsky); Bristol Bridge in autumn (Brizzleboy); Church Avenue in spring (Linda Bailey); Castle Park in summer (Steinsky)

30. Bristol Ferry (Rod Ward)

31. St Nicholas' Market lights (NotFromUtrecht); The Old Duke, King Street (Stephen Burnett)

33. Cumberland Basin (Steinsky); Bristol city centre in summer (Fig Wright); Traffic congestion around Cabot Circus (mattbuck); Clifton Suspension Bridge by night (Cako)

34. St John's Gate (Doris Ogilvie, kindly uploaded and cleared by her son, user name Duncanogi at en.wikipedia); Broad Street in recent years (Rodhullandemu)

35. St Mary Redcliffe (*Bristol Past & Present*); the same in 2006 (Matt Gibson)

37. Bristol city centre (William J. Bagshaw); postcard of city centre (Garratt); Floating Harbour (Richard Pearson)

38-39. Bristol Temple Meads station (Rwendland); Bristol panorama (Klafubra)

41. Charles Kingsley (Frederick Waddy); Shakespeare (Library of Congress, Prints & Photographs Division, LC-USZ61-214); Jim and Long John Silver from a 1911 edition of *Treasure Island;* The *Hispaniola* (George Roux)

42. Noel Coward and Lillian Braithwaite (Library of Congress, Prints & Photographs Division, Carl Van Vechten Collection, LC-DIG-ggbain-38534); Cary Grant (THP)

43. Roald Dahl and Patricia Neal (Library of Congress, Prints & Photographs Division, Carl Van Vechten Collection, LC-USZ62-54231)

45. Bristol blue glass (Adrian Pingstone); Cabot Tower (Adrian Pingstone); Gromit scarecrow (Acather96)

46. A slave coffle passing the Capitol (Library of Congress, Prints & Photographs Division, LC-USZ62-2574); harvesting tobacco (Library of Congress, Prints & Photographs Division, LC-DIG-nclc-00448)

49. Newsvendor (Library of Congress, Prints & Photographs Division, LC-DIG-ppmsc-08046)

50-51. College Green (Library of Congress, Prints & Photographs Division, LC-DIG-ppmsc-08046)

53. Blaise Castle (Michiel Jelijs); SS *Great Britain* (Mike Peel, www.mikepeel.net); Bristol City Museum (Steinsky); Arnolfini (Linda Bailey)

55. Arnos Vale (Adrian Pingstone)

57. Llandoger Trow (*Bristol Past & Present*)

59. Fishmarket (Rod Ward); Everard works (Jongleur100)

61. St Nicholas Market (*Bristol Past & Present*)

62. Bristol Council House (Green Lane); Colston Hall (Ben Mills); Bristol Cathedral (NotFromUtrecht)

63. Feeder Canal industrial buildings (mattbuck); All Saints' church, south side (NotFromUtrecht); Back of King Street pubs (Jezhotwells)

64. Italianate building, Victoria Street (William Avery); New development at harbourside (Linda Bailey); King Street, south side (NotFromUtrecht); University of Bristol's Medical Buildings (Francium12)

65. Corn Street old bank (Chaps the idol); Bristol Old Vic gallery (Rob Brewer)

66-67. River Avon from the Downs (Library of Congress, Prints & Photographs Division, LC-DIG-ppmsc-08053)

69. Wild Service Tree (Andrew Dunn, www.andrewdunnphoto.com); Veronica Spicata (masaki ikeda); swans on the Avon (Rob Brewer); fallow deer (Adrian Pingstone)

71. Brandon Hill (Steinsky); Snuff Mills bridge (William Avery)

73. Balloon Festival 2000 (MattBallooning); Wills cigarette card issued by Imperial Tobacco; MoD, Filton (Adrian Pingstone); Airbus A380 (Tino 'Scorpi' Keitel, Bearbeiter, Johann H. Addicks, jha)

75. Police (Library of Congress, Prints & Photographs Division, LC-USZ62-28517); fire (Library of Congress, Prints & Photographs Division, LC-USZ62-25570); doctor (Library of Congress, Prints & Photographs Division, LC-USZ62-54106)

77. Revamping of the Bristol & West building (Rob Brewer); Bristol Royal Infirmary (Linda Bailey); The Swan Boat floating restaurant (Rodw)

79. Plaque (Andrew Dingley); Sir Michael Redgrave (Allan Warren)

81. Statue of Bevin (HarveyW001); statue of Nelson's column (Library of Congress, Prints & Photographs Division, LC-USZ62-120649)

83. Hannah More plaque (Rodw); Norah Cooke-Hurle plaque (Rodw); Mary Carpenter (Chris Heaton)

85. Paul Boateng (wy_harvard)

89. Edward Kelly invoking a spirit (FromOldBooks.com)

HILLSIDE GUIDES - ACROSS THE NORTH

Yorkshire River Photobooks •JOURNEY OF THE WHARFE

Easy Walks •50 YORKSHIRE WALKS FOR ALL

Walking in Yorkshire - North/East (25 Walks)
•NORTH YORK MOORS South/West   •NORTH YORK MOORS North/East
•YORKSHIRE WOLDS   •HOWARDIAN HILLS & VALE OF YORK

Walking in Yorkshire - West/South/Mid (25 Walks)
•AIRE VALLEY & BRONTE COUNTRY   •HARROGATE & ILKLEY
•CALDERDALE & SOUTH PENNINES   •SOUTH YORKSHIRE
•WEST YORKSHIRE COUNTRYSIDE

Walking in Yorkshire - Yorkshire Dales (25 Walks)
•East: NIDDERDALE & RIPON   •West: THREE PEAKS & HOWGILL FELLS
•South: WHARFEDALE & MALHAM   •North: WENSLEYDALE & SWALEDALE

Circular Walks - Lancashire/North West/North Pennines
•BOWLAND   •PENDLE & the RIBBLE   •ARNSIDE & SILVERDALE
•EDEN VALLEY   •ALSTON & ALLENDALE

Long Distance Walks
•COAST TO COAST WALK •DALES WAY •CUMBRIA WAY •PENDLE WAY

Hillwalking - Lake District (25 Walks)
•LAKELAND FELLS - SOUTH   •LAKELAND FELLS - EAST
•LAKELAND FELLS - NORTH   •LAKELAND FELLS - WEST

Short Scenic Walks (30 Walks)
•NORTH YORK MOORS   •HARROGATE & NIDDERDALE
•AMBLESIDE & SOUTH LAKELAND   •WHARFEDALE & ILKLEY

Short Scenic Walks (20 Walks)
•SWALEDALE   •UPPER WENSLEYDALE   •LOWER WENSLEYDALE
•INGLETON & WESTERN DALES   •RIBBLESDALE   •MALHAMDALE
•SEDBERGH & DENTDALE   •HEBDEN BRIDGE
•AIRE VALLEY   •HAWORTH & BRONTE COUNTRY
•AROUND PENDLE   •RIBBLE VALLEY   •BOWLAND

*Send for a detailed current catalogue and price list
and also visit www.hillsidepublications.co.uk*

WALKING in YORKSHIRE

—

WEST YORKSHIRE
COUNTRYSIDE

Paul Hannon

—

Hillside

HILLSIDE PUBLICATIONS

2 New School Lane
Cullingworth
Bradford
West Yorkshire
BD13 5DA

First published 2020

© Paul Hannon 2020   ISBN 978-1-907626-22-7

Cover illustrations: Leeds-Liverpool Canal at Newlay; Roundhay Park
Back cover: Thornton Viaduct; Page One: Calder & Hebble at Mirfield
Page Three: Norwood Green; Above: Yorkshire Sculpture Park
Opposite: Almshouses at Ledsham
(Paul Hannon/Yorkshire Photo Library)

The sketch maps are based on 1947 Ordnance Survey One-Inch maps

Printed in China on behalf of Latitude Press

CONTENTS

INTRODUCTION

West Yorkshire hosts numerous dense conurbations, from the cities of Leeds, Bradford and Wakefield to countless towns such as Huddersfield, Halifax, Keighley, Dewsbury and Castleford. This book showcases the remarkable variety of walking opportunities on the doorsteps of these towns and cities, ranging from attractive dormitory villages to canal towpaths and semi-urban parks. The western and northern parts of West Yorkshire are famed for the rolling moors and dales of the Pennines, a hilly region featured in the companion guides *Aire Valley & Bronte Country*, *Calderdale & South Pennines* and part of *Harrogate & Ilkley*. With the Bradford, Halifax (Calderdale) and Huddersfield (Kirklees) districts largely covered in those three volumes, this guide effectively embraces the eastern half of West Yorkshire, with the mighty city of Leeds at its hub.

Flowing from the Pennines are the two principal rivers of the Aire and the Calder, which join forces at Castleford: both are encountered in their broader lower reaches. In tandem with them, a major feature of the district is its canals, built over 200 years ago to provide an efficient means of transporting goods between the communities. While the Leeds-Liverpool and Barnsley canals were purpose-built for barges, the Aire & Calder and Calder & Hebble Navigations were created to augment the rivers, offering short-cuts to avoid weirs and time-consuming bends. Heavy commercial use of the canal age was short-lived as the railways rapidly replaced them, and today the towpaths of these waterways offer endless opportunities for the most genteel of rambling, usually decorated by brightly coloured barges of the modern leisure age.

Other historic transport settings include old railways at Thornton Viaduct, Queensbury Tunnel and the Chevet Branch Line. Packhorse trails are followed at Judy Woods, Shadwell and Tong, while flavours of the Great North Road are rekindled at Aberford and Fairburn. Ancient castle sites are visited at Barwick in Elmet and Bardsey, with Iron Age defensive earthworks at Aberford and monastic iron workings at Emley. Magnificent old houses dominate extensive parkland at Temple Newsam and Oakwell Hall, while richly characterful villages include Ledsham, Heath and Woolley.

WALKING in YORKSHIRE

WEST YORKSHIRE COUNTRYSIDE

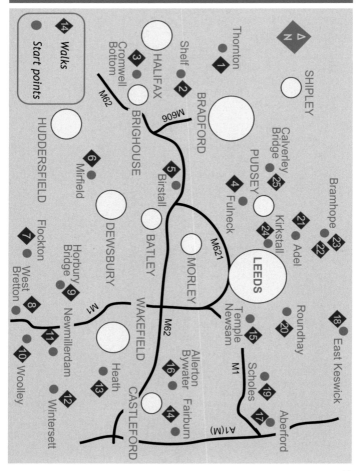

◆ 14 Walks

● Start points

7

INTRODUCTION

Fascinating nature reserves of the RSPB occupy former coal mining sites in lower Airedale, remarkably transformed scenes where industry has been replaced by nature at Allerton Bywater and Fairburn. Wildlife also flourishes at the reservoirs at Wintersett, Newmillerdam and Eccup, and the latter's location on the fringes of the Wharfe Valley see the skies above regularly patrolled by enigmatic Red kites. Substantial climbing cliffs are met at Hetchell Crags and Becca Banks Crag, and ornamental lakes at Roundhay, Golden Acre and Bretton parks. Other, more individual, highlights of the landscape include Emley Moor, Kirkstall Abbey, Fulneck's Moravian settlement and the hugely absorbing Yorkshire Sculpture Park.

Using the guide

The walks range from 5 to 7½ miles, with the average distance being around 6 miles. Each walk is self-contained, with essential information being followed by a concise route description and a simple map. Dovetailed in between are snippets of information on features along the way: these are placed in *italics* to ensure that the all important route description is easier to locate. Start point postcodes are a rough guide only for those with 'satnav': grid references are more precise!

The sketch maps serve to identify the location of the routes rather than the fine detail, and whilst the description should be sufficient to guide you around, the appropriate Ordnance Survey map is recommended. To gain the most from a walk, the detail of a 1:25,000 scale Explorer map is unsurpassed. It also gives the option to vary walks as desired, giving a much improved picture of your surroundings and the availability of any linking paths for shortening or lengthening walks. Four maps cover all the walks:
- *Explorer 278 - Sheffield & Barnsley*
- *Explorer 288 - Bradford & Huddersfield*
- *Explorer 289 - Leeds*
- *Explorer 297 - Lower Wharfedale & Washburn Valley*

Also very useful for planning are Landranger maps 104 and 110.

Information Centres
Visitleeds, The Headrow **Leeds** LS1 3AA • 0113-3786977
Treacy Hall, Wakefield Cathedral **Wakefield** WF1 1HG • 0845-6018353
City Hall, Centenary Square **Bradford** BD1 1HY • 01274-433678
Library, Princess Alexandra Walk **Huddersfield** HD1 2SU • 01484-223200
The Piece Hall, Blackledge **Halifax** HX1 1RE • 01422-368725

Opposite: At Bramhope   *Cornfield above Mirfield*

AROUND THORNTON

Ups and downs galore outside of this hilltop village

START *Thornton (SE 105327; BD13 3AB)*

DISTANCE *6$\frac{1}{2}$ miles (10$\frac{1}{2}$km)*

ORDNANCE SURVEY 1:25,000 MAP
Explorer 288 - Bradford & Huddersfield

ACCESS *Start from parish church on B6145 Bradford-Keelham road, roadside parking. Bus from Bradford and Keighley.*

Thornton retains a defiant independence from its lofty perch above Bradford. St James' spired church of 1870 looks across the road to a churchyard with the remains of the Bell Chapel that was the parish church when the Rev Patrick Bronte arrived in 1815. Market Street features Kipping Chapel of 1843 and the former parsonage, numbers 72 and 74, where Bronte and his wife Maria spent five years. During this time their famous offspring were born: Charlotte (1816), Branwell (1817), Emily (1818) and Anne (1820). From the church head east towards Bradford, but just past the old churchyard turn down a short rough road serving Thornton Hall. Before its gates go left a few strides on a green way, where a kissing-gate on the right puts you into a field corner with big valley views. A path slants left down this rolling field to a bottom corner stile. Through it a short path runs through trees to a cart track at what was Corn Mill Farm: follow its lane the short way out over Pinch Beck onto Chat Hill Road.

Go left a few strides and then right along Low Lane. Just after the roads merge, cross Hole Bottom Beck and escape into a field by a stile/gate on the right. Head away with the tree-lined stream on your right, and ignoring an old wall going left, advance further to a gateway at the next old wall. Bear left to follow this uphill, crossing to its left side to rise to a stile in the top corner. *Look back across the valley to Thornton dominated by its church spire. Further left is Thornton Viaduct, which you shall later be crossing.*

An enclosed path continues up the fieldside to a gap at the top onto the end of an enclosed path on the edge of Clayton. Don't use it, but turn right through the gate, and the continuing path rises a few feet to head away with the wall above. Through a stile you reach an old quarried area at Hanging Fall, and

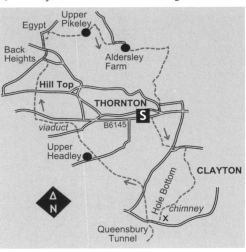

the path slants pleasantly down to the next gap, maintaining this line along the base of a spoil heap from Fall Top Quarry. Continue on with an old wall, and past a solitary tree, pass through the wall and drop right with the facing wall a short way to a stile in it. Resume along a field bottom to the next stile ahead, and the path crosses a sloping field centre to the next stile. Now drop gently across to a gap in the wall ahead beneath a gate that you don't use. It continues down across the slope to another stile. *En route you glimpse an old chimney at Clayton Fire Clay Works, supposedly decorated to celebrate Bradford City's FA Cup victory in 1911.* The path runs on beneath further workings just above the valley floor of Hole Bottom, through an old gateway to a stile onto Brow Lane.

Turn right for the short pull to a tall railway arch. Immediately under, a firm path rises left onto a surfaced path on the old line at the edge of Queensbury's old station. Though your onward route is left, first advance two minutes right to Queensbury Triangle. Through the first gate a right turn sends a broad path on the old line through trees to Queensbury Tunnel's northern portal. *Completed in 1878 by the Great Northern Railway to link Halifax, Bradford and Keighley, the line was dubbed the 'Alpine Route' in deference to its viaducts and tunnels. Though a great engineering feat to bring a railway to this altitude from the surrounding towns, construction and running costs were always a major headache, and the line closed in 1956. Fast forward to 2020, and on going to press its future hangs in the balance: a magnificent walking/cycle path, or filled in forever?*

Returning along the tarmac path, it crosses the bridge you passed under and rises away with glimpses of the chimney to your right. The way drop back down past a derelict house to Cocking Lane, the path veering right a few paces to cross. Resume opposite to join an access road, which runs on beneath a tall footbridge to end at a house on the left. *Big views look right to Thornton and down to Bradford.* A tarmac path returns, running through greenery over an embankment on the idyllic side valley of High Birks Beck. Another steeply climbing road is met just beyond, and again cross straight over. Passing beneath a substantial stone bridge you are rapidly upon the mighty Thornton Viaduct. *Up to 120ft high, its 20 arches carried the line across the valley of Pinch Beck. At the other side a right fork offers a much shorter finish back into Thornton.*

The main route swings left past a school, with a view back to the viaduct. *Immediately after the school grounds is the site of Thornton station: just a little further west the old line disappears into Well Heads Tunnel, through which the railway burrowed 662 yards towards Denholme.* On through School Wood it swings right at the end, abandoning the line to enter a housing development at Woodsley Fold. Head away briefly along Rowlands Close, and on meeting a T-junction just ahead, go right a few strides to leave by a path rising left up steps onto the B6145. From a stile opposite, an enclosed path climbs a field edge outside a cemetery. Crossing a level access path, resume uphill to a top corner stile. Advance to a kissing-gate ahead, and a short enclosed path runs on to emerge onto Hill Top Road, with the Ring o'Bells pub on your left.

The onward route goes straight across to enter a private-looking yard, and a flagged path runs on to emerge via a stile into a field. A path advances straight on with the wall on your right. *At some 1050ft/320m this high point of the walk offers massive views north, far beyond Rombalds Moor to Great Whernside at the top of Wharfedale.* This straight line is maintained as the path becomes enclosed at the end, a series of gap-stiles taking the enclosed path through, over a path crossroads and along to a final stile into an open field. Advance away, bearing slightly left to a brow overlooking a house in a quarried hollow. Bear right a short way along this rim to a flight of stone steps dropping to a wall by the entrance gate. A one-sided stile takes you down onto the drive, which runs out the few strides onto Upper Heights Road at Back Heights.

At the junction with Back Heights Road on your left, turn right down Rock Lane to the Rock & Heifer pub. Go left a few strides on Lower Heights Road alongside it (becoming Black Dyke Lane), then turn right down Egypt Road alongside cottages, with the Old Stone Mill on your left. Part way down, take a flight of steps along the near side of cottages on the right. It swings left as a snicket outside them to then drop steeply to emerge along-side further houses at Egypt, rejoining the road alongside them. *Back to your left at an abandoned hairpin bend once stood the celebrated Walls of Jericho: these enormous 19th century stone walls were built to retain spoil from quarries, but sadly were demolished in 1985 on safety grounds.*

Thornton church and Bell Chapel remains

13

Advance a few strides along the road in this dip, then take a path climbing steps between old walls on your right. Through an old stile at the top it quickly meets a broader way just above, turning right along this above the colourful valley head of Bell Dean. This level path makes a nice stroll, largely with a wall on your left. Soon passing between wider spaced walls you emerge into a field, and the fading grassy way points to a corner stile. This sends a path on outside house grounds, through a further stile and along a grassy area to join the drive to Upper Pikeley. Advance briefly along it as far as some sheds, where a stile on the right sends an enclosed path down a fieldside. Through small gates you emerge lower down to continue with the wall to a corner gate guarding a stile onto an access road at Lower Pikeley. Turn left to a junction with Long Lane, and go right on Upper Allerton Lane, dropping down past houses at Allerton Upper Green. Swinging right, the surfaced road ends just short of 17th century Aldersley Farm.

Remain on the rough road dropping left past houses: between buildings at the end it becomes a walled cart track running to a gate into a small field. It crosses to a gate into the wooded confines of a streamlet, ignoring a gate to the right. Fording the stream, it rises back out into the open, and fades. Ignore the fence-gate just ahead, and bear slightly right to cross the field top to locate a gap-stile in the very corner. Head away with the wall on your right to rise to a gate at a wall corner ahead. *Just visible up to your left is historic Lower Bailey Fold Farm amid new housing on the edge of Allerton*. Through this descend with the wall on your left, briefly, with a big view over the valley to Thornton.

As the wall turns away, simply descend the field with an old hedge-line: part way down as two old walls diverge, follow the right one pointing towards the stream of Pitty Beck in the bottom. Across a double stone slab footbridge, just a few yards downstream is a stile in the old wall/fence to your right. Ascend two steep fieldsides to a gate at the top corner. Pass through and go left the short way on an enclosed cart track to a gate/stile in front of houses at Hoyle Ing House. Head away on the access road between the houses, out onto the bend of a suburban street in Thornton. Advance to a T-junction and turn right. Shortly take the branch left, soon arriving at a snicket which runs left between gardens back onto the main road alongside the church.

14

JUDY WOODS

Extensive woodland and a lovely village of broad greens

START *Shelf (SE 122282; HX3 7NT)*

DISTANCE *5^{1}4 miles (8^{1}2km)*

ORDNANCE SURVEY 1:25,000 MAP
Explorer 288 - Bradford & Huddersfield

ACCESS *Start from Bridle Stile car park just off A6036
through Shelf at Shelf Hall Park. Bradford-Halifax bus.*

From the car park entrance turn down the continuing lane of Bridle Stile, losing its surface and emerging into open fields. *En route, sections of paving of the original road are seen, its grooved centres worn by cartwheels.* At the bottom you arrive at Dean House: without entering the farm take a stile on the right and then immediately over one on the left. Descend the field outside the grounds, then down more steeply to a footbridge on Wood Fall Beck. Entering North Wood the path bears right, and quickly forking, the onward route slants up the bank. First however, a magnificent waterfall just a minute downstream is seen by striding the beck just above it to run a few yards around to a prime vantage point.

The onward route quickly rises to a path junction to run right along the wood top, and soon leaves the trees to slant faintly up a field to the top corner. Through the gap the path runs on the field-side to enter an enclosed way. Advance straight on to emerge at an access road-end at Middle Ox Heys. Follow the drive out onto Norwood Green Hill at Norwood Green. Go left up to the brow and cross to tiny Chapel Street onto open ground. *This lovely village is graced with several extensive greens: alongside you is the Ellis Memorial Clock Tower of 1897, centrepiece of a private garden.*

Across the small green a footpath delves into greenery: ignoring a branch path dropping to the right,

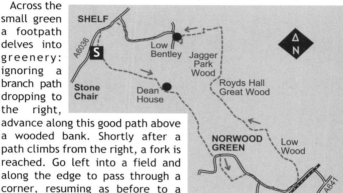

advance along this good path above a wooded bank. Shortly after a path climbs from the right, a fork is reached. Go left into a field and along the edge to pass through a corner, resuming as before to a gate/gap by a house. Advance on the short access road back into the village on a spacious green. *Along to the left is the Old White Beare, an old pub recalling a ship that helped halt the Spanish Armada in 1588.* Cross this to rejoin the road and go right, past further greens to pass the Pear Tree pub and descend Station Road out of the village.

After it swings left at the bottom, take a stile into trees at the start of Low Wood. The extensive woodland you are entering is known locally as Judy Woods. A broad path heads away to a big embankment over Royd Hall Beck. Across, keep left on the broad, main path slanting gently left uphill. It runs a grand course above the steep drop to the beck, and on for some time in similar vein to merge with a firmer path from the right where a fence forces you right to a gateway. This junction with an old lane is an historic packhorse way you will briefly follow. Turn left down an enclosed path alongside the lane to merge at the bottom in front of stone-arched Horse Close Bridge, more popularly known as Judy's Brig.

Don't cross but take the path upstream into Royds Hall Great Wood. Quickly forking, ignore the steeper, stepped path right and advance straight on, up a few steps and resuming upstream through the wood. From here on are a number of lesser variations, though the principal route is identified by a reasonably regular set of low, red-banded marker posts. The path largely remains close by but above the beck in its deep 'ravine', and undulates along for quite some time, joined by a path from the right and passing through intriguing hummocks. At an easily missed fork it drops slightly left to another, immediate fork where it sends you slightly back uphill. Though sometimes thinner and sometimes nearer the beck, the general direction remains the same and you shouldn't go far wrong.

Just after passing beneath power lines, ignore a tempting drop to the beck itself: your way bears right, climbing briefly steeply to a welcome bench on a brow. Now resume left, extremely high above the deep valley with fields just over to the right. Again a firmer main path runs parallel to your right, and again your best way remains closer to the drop, a superb stride through stately beeches. Latterly it rises very gently and runs to the wood edge where the paths merge. Pass through a kissing-gate out into a rough enclosure, and advance the short way to another sending a surfaced path into modern housing. Ignore this, and take a short path left to an old gateway overlooking a scrubby bank outside the wood edge. The path drops down this towards the beck, then runs briefly upstream above it to drop to cross it. A few steps up the other side see the path rising right across this steep, wooded bank, then up a larger flight of steps before running more gently on Doubling briefly back left, it rises onto a broad path along the valley edge. Pass through a stile in front and head away along fieldsides to Low Bentley. The path is deflected left outside the grounds, becoming enclosed to swing round to join a cart track rising onto surfaced Green Lane outside this fine house of 1600.

Turn right on the roadside footway, keeping left at an early junction and on past increasing modern housing. At the end it swings right as Brow Lane outside Royds Hall Wood's uppermost confines. After Brow Wood Rise on the right, bear left on a short access road that narrows to a snicket, passing a stone pinfold and up steep steps back onto the A6036. Go left on the footway for a few minutes past an industrial site, with the Bottomleys Arms and the long terrace of Spring Head opposite. Reaching a lodge at old gateposts to Shelf Hall, enter the park to cross to the car park.

ELLAND PARK WOOD

Splendid woodland paths from towpath to hilltop hamlet

START *Cromwell Bottom (SE 124223; HD6 2RG)*

DISTANCE *5½ miles (8¾km)*

ORDNANCE SURVEY 1:25,000 MAP
Explorer 288 - Bradford & Huddersfield

ACCESS *Start from Cromwell Bottom nature reserve car park off A6026 Elland Road west of Brighouse. Brighouse-Elland bus.*

From the end of the car park cross the pedestrian bridge alongside Crowther Bridge, and drop left onto the towpath of the Calder & Hebble Navigation. Turn right (away from the bridge) to commence a pleasant stroll on the surfaced path all the way to Brookfoot Bridge in front of a large factory at Brookfoot Mills. En route you have the option to explore the nature reserve on your right, with several gates accessing the site. *The River Calder flows to your right at the start and the end, while across the canal a large lake hosts water-skiers on the site of old gravel pits.* The towpath passes under rusting Freeman's Bridge and alongside Cromwell Bridge and Lock, a lovely spot, before a dead-straight run to Brookfoot Bridge and Lock. *Here stands Brookfoot Lock Lobby, a former lock-keeper's cottage, while to your left is a fishery.*

Cross the canal bridge and advance a short way along the broad path to North Cut access road at stone-arched Camms Mill

Bridge. Go left the short way to the A6026. Cross to a stile sending the broad path of Cromwell Wood Lane slanting left with a wall up through Freeman's Wood, with springtime bluebells. After a steady rise it levels out, with a fork just ahead. Keep to the level left branch with the wall, soon rising gently to a sharp bend in front of two stiles at the wood edge. *Unseen just above are Cromwell Quarries, with the lake well seen below.* From the left-hand stile a near immediate descent begins: steepening and then enclosed by walls, it is a remarkable if frustrating adventure. Over 250 not unkindly steep steps descend to the rear of Fort Montague Farm. By this stage you are virtually back on the valley floor, though compensation is to be found in the contrastingly genteel re-ascent.

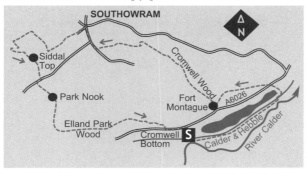

Turn right on the splendid, walled green way of Wood Lane to enter Cromwell Wood. A path begins a mercurial rise, ever gently up through silver birch and oak woodland, with an older sunken way in tandem much of the way. Ignoring any branches, eventually it becomes enclosed at the top, rising still to a path crossroads in an open area. With Southowram just above, go left on a setted way to curve round the very head of the clough, through a stile and along to an access road. Go right just yards, then from a stile on the left a long fieldside path rises to approach a suburban scene.

From the top corner stile an enclosed path emerges onto an access road, School Lane, with attractive Jerusalem Square on your right. Go straight ahead to join Ashday Lane and turn right into Southowram at Town Gate. Keep right past the village stocks and a shop to a five-way junction by the Pack Horse pub. Take suburban

Yeadon Drive doubling back left outside a lodge, and soon ending with a gateway/stile in front. A flagged wallside path heads away, and from a stile at the end, continue this faintest of rises alongside a fence. Through a stile at the top you gain the walk's high point: advance with a wall to the next stile just ahead, and pause on this brow to survey the newly revealed panorama ahead. *This features an extensive Pennine skyline from Black Hill around to Ovenden Moor, with Halifax and the Wainhouse Tower in front of you.*

Resume down the field centre to an old wall, then advance to the wall just in front and go right to a stile in this tapering corner. Resume along the wall-top, with the old house of Backhold Royd below. Through another stile continue on to one onto an enclosed track. Go left, now just a grassy pathway dropping to a viewpoint corner below. The way then swings left to drop onto a driveway, doubling back right on it the short way onto unsurfaced Siddal Top Lane. Go left on this for a steady stroll, curving up through the hamlet of Siddal Wells. After a steep little pull it runs on to emerge onto a road, West Lane. Go right a few strides on the footway, and cross to an unsurfaced access road at Westfield Gate. This runs past houses and a farm to end at the secluded hamlet of Park Nook. In front of the last house, a stile on the right sends a path slanting down a field to a gate/gap below, overlooking a colourful scrubby bowl. Of the grassy paths heading away, take the left one rising slightly to a gateway into Elland Park Wood.

Within yards a cross-paths is met: bear right on that dropping gently away, soon easing to run a level course to the left beneath bluebell banks. At a fork remain on the level path, soon merging into one rising from the right. Bear left up this, rapidly easing to commence a generally level course along a broad, hummocky shelf beneath much steeper slopes. Ignoring any branch paths, it later drops very gently, then on beneath a craggy bluff and a pond where it forks. Bear left uphill, again briefly, and through an old wall-gap to soon arrive at a hairpin bend on the firmer old way of Binns Top Lane. Turn right, dropping gently all the way through Binns Wood. At the bottom it emerges onto an access road in front of two houses at Near Binns. Go right on this driveway down to a junction, with the A6026 rejoined just to your right. Turn left on the footway for the remaining five minutes back to the start, crossing to turn down the access road back to the car park.

COCKERS DALE & TONG

Streamside paths and old packhorse trails

START *Fulneck (SE 216320; LS28 8EB)*

DISTANCE *6 miles (9$\frac{1}{2}$km)*

ORDNANCE SURVEY 1:25,000 MAP
Explorer 288 - Bradford & Huddersfield

ACCESS *Start from Bankhouse pub at end of Bankhouse Lane,
south of Pudsey. Roadside parking, notably on lane above pub.*

Established in 1744 by a community from Moravia (now in the
Czech Republic), the settlement at Fulneck sits on the edge of the
busy town of Pudsey. It includes a splendid chapel and school among
many fine buildings and cottages overlooking the rural valley of
Pudsey Beck. Facing the pub, go left beneath its car park along an
access road the short way to the private gates of Nesbit Hall. Here,
by a stone trough and spring, a path takes a kissing-gate on the
right up into a field. It quickly bears right to ascend the centre to
a wall-stile marking the start of a splendid enclosed path. This rises
very gently to reveal Pudsey church tower from the brow, then
drops the short way onto the suburban street of Greentop. Cross
straight over and down a short snicket onto Smalewell Road.

Go left, and at the end take a bridleway left down the near
side of the Fox & Grapes pub. Leaving suburbia behind with open views
over Pudsey Beck's valley, it slants gently down into Black Carr

21

Wood. *Note a tunnel entrance on the left and embankment on the right from the Great Northern Railway's Pudsey & Low Moor branch.* Further, ignore a thinner path branching right, and at the bottom the bridleway doubles back right to a ford and stepping-stones. Ignore this in favour of a stile ahead to commence a splendid amble downstream with Pudsey Beck to your right. Ignoring an early footbridge, this remains unchanged for some time. Soon after emerging into a clearing you join Scholebrook Lane, a hard track.

Go briefly right towards the beck, but take a stile on the left to resume downstream across a grassy pasture amid pleasant open surroundings. On beneath a flowery bank you meet the meandering beck again, and through a gap-stile into trees. A spell tight by the beck precedes arrival at a path junction by a footbridge, ford and stepping-stones - you will return here near the end. Don't cross the beck, but resume downstream on the path breaking into the open to run an invisible course between Fulneck golf course and the beck. At the end you run briefly through scrub to a stile into open pasture. South Park Mill is soon passed up to your left as the path stays tight by the beck to emerge by way of a kissing-gate into a large pasture. A steady stroll on the base of sloping pastures ultimately leads to being enclosed alongside the beck once again. Your path soon emerges via a snicket onto the wide road of Roker Lane.

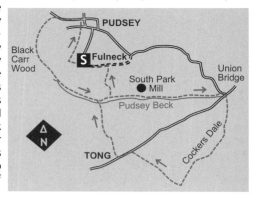

Drop right on the footway alongside the converted Union Bridge Mill to a T-junction, and cross straight over to a broad path into trees. Don't rush off, but immediately leave the bridleway in favour of a broad path right through a kissing-gate. This runs a super course upstream with Tong Beck into Cockers Dale. Remain on the main path until a little beyond a wooden bridge over a streamlet, where fork right to a footbridge on the beck. A path ascends the other bank to a kissing-gate into a field corner. It runs left along the field bottom above trees, and on to enter scattered trees and undergrowth: a gate at the end returns you closer to the beck. Passing a wooden farm bridge and cattle ford, the briefly broader way curves up to the right, but remain with the beck to a small gate by a footbridge. Through further trees to another small gate, the path then runs on the base of a sloping pasture before a kissing-gate back into trees. A final pasture precedes arrival at a bridleway at a small arched bridge on a kink of the beck.

Don't cross the bridge but turn right up the hollowed way of Springfield Lane, which commences a long but very gentle climb out of the valley. *The neighbourhood of Tong boasts a network of packhorse routes by which traders – or 'jaggers' - would lead trains of horses laden with goods from town to town and farm to farm. Both Springfield Lane and later Keeper Lane have sections of stone causeway - or causey – which provided a firmer footing for ponies.* The path eases out further as Tong is revealed, then broadens in its upper stages to enter the village at its eastern end. *This attractive street village occupies a lofty ridge amid an extensive rural setting. St James' church of 1727 has stocks outside, while set back close by is brick-built Tong Hall of 1702. The Greyhound pub stands among characterful old houses, while on entering the village you pass an ice cream establishment.*

Cross and go left on the footway into the village. Just before the pub and cricket pitch, turn right on surfaced Keeper Lane at a pinfold and pump. This rises away past the 17th century Manor House and ends where an enclosed bridleway takes over at a gate. Here commence a sustained descent to the valley bottom, largely with the line of a causey. At the bottom are the earlier footbridge, ford and stepping-stones on Pudsey Beck. Across, turn right on your earlier path by the golf course, but this time take the signed option rising left past an island tree to the start of a path into trees above. This ascends a largely unbroken, flagged course through trees, then up between hedges with the golf course to either side. At the top you emerge between school buildings onto an access road, with a through road just above. With the main body of the school to your right, go left past a tearoom in the original shop of 1762. A raised pavement leads to a grassy bank which is crossed to the pub.

SHIRLEY COUNTRY

Absorbing rambling above the Spen Valley

START Birstall (SE 217270; WF17 9LG)

DISTANCE 6½ miles (10½km)

ORDNANCE SURVEY 1:25,000 MAP
Explorer 288 - Bradford & Huddersfield

ACCESS Start from Oakwell Hall car park off A652 between
Birstall and Birkenshaw. Bradford-Dewsbury bus on main road.

Oakwell Hall is an Elizabethan manor house built by the Batt
family, and visitors can enter within its gritstone walls to glimpse
the lifestyle of a well-to-do family of that period. Charlotte Bronte
featured it as Fieldhead in 'Shirley'. Managed by Kirklees Council,
it is at the heart of a country park in the shadow of the M62, with
an information centre, café and shop in the adjacent courtyard. In
1643 the Battle of Adwalton Moor was fought less than a mile
north, with Parliamentarian forces retreating past Oakwell Hall.

From the hall front, head down the short drive to the car park
entrance and gates onto Nutter Lane. Cross straight over onto a
broad, enclosed path descending between equestrian pastures to a
stone bridge accessing the A652. Cross the road and along suburban
Monk Ings. As it swings round to the right, take a rough road left
between houses after Friary Court. At the end a stile by a gate
sends a faint path rising gently up the fields, linked by kissing-

gates. Rising further, bear right towards a clump of trees, and through an old gateway the now enclosed path runs between hedges, and right outside a burial ground into modern housing. Rise away, swinging left as Scott Lane out onto the A651 at Gomersal. *A United Reformed Church stands to the left.*

Cross by pedestrian lights at the school to the Public Hall, then into a car park at the rear of the Red House. *Dating from 1660, it is named from its bright, red-brick exterior in an otherwise stone-built district. Charlotte Bronte regularly visited her friend Mary Taylor here, and the house featured as Briarmains in 'Shirley'. Until 2016 it was a museum in the flavour of the Taylor's and Bronte's era.* Cross the grassy area behind the car park to a wall-gap into a snicket in front of modern housing. Go left on this long, tightly enclosed footway onto the A643 almost opposite Gomersal church. Cross and go right to the far end, then left on Shirley Road.

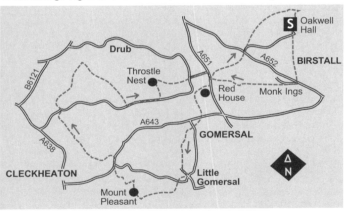

The churchyard path offers an alternative short-cut at the front and out via a gate at the far corner, with far-reaching views to the west. St Mary's is a large, imposing building with a fine west tower: Mary Taylor's gravestone can be seen on the western side, by the churchyard wall. Go left along Shirley Road, but almost at once turn right on Butts Hill. After the first houses on the left, a cinder path breaks off left through a small gateway to run the length of an unkempt tract of scrubby ground. Emerging at the end into more open surrounds, remain on the path straight ahead, over a cross-paths and on the diminishing bank with a football pitch to your left. At the end a path from the pitch comes in, and ignoring a left branch into woodland, advance fifty yards further to a path dropping right the few yards to a seat at Nibshaw Lane.

Go left into Little Gomersal. Ahead is a broad junction at Town Hill Square, but your route is right on cul-de-sac Parkside into the Wheatsheaf pub car park. *Its rear appearance belies its attractive frontage and interior.* If not visiting, take a snicket right of the car park the short way onto Gomersal Lane. *This reveals spacious views over the Spen Valley to Emley Moor TV mast, while further right are the north-eastern moors of the Peak District above Meltham. Dwarfed beneath the skyline is the Victoria tower on Castle Hill.*

Just a couple of yards right, take a stile by the right-hand gate opposite and a path descends the fieldside. Through a gate/stile at the bottom, turn right on a track along the field top to another gate/stile. Take the left-hand path across the field, dropping at the corner to a hedge-stile onto a rough access road. Go right the short way towards Mount Pleasant, and the path is deflected right on a briefly enclosed course to join a drive at the other side. Advance on briefly past the small cluster of houses, then take an enclosed path dropping left to a gate into a field. Drop right to a stile/gate in the bottom corner, then down the next fieldside the short way to a corner stile beneath an old railway embankment. The enclosed path runs beneath the bank, broadening to rise the short way onto the A643 alongside an old rail bridge.

Go briefly right past a road end, then cross and head off on a rough access road. Quickly leave this at an unkempt industrial area by a tarmac path left: this runs the short way to a wooded bank above Mann Dam Reservoir. *To your left, the tall, frail-looking Mann Dam Viaduct carried an access road from Cleckheaton Spen station into the nearby town centre.* Take the broad path right, descending pleasantly through the wood to run along the bottom a short way to the wood end. At the path junction turn left along the edge of the wood to emerge alongside reedbeds. Advance the short way to a path junction at the end, then take the raised walkway right alongside further reedbeds in the valley bottom. Emerging at the end, advance along a fenceside to cross to a bridge on the River Spen. A flagged path crosses an open area on the edge of suburbia.

At the path junction ahead, re-cross the stream and a surfaced path shadows a sidestream the short way up onto a bend of Cliffe Lane. Go briefly left to the next bend and take a snicket straight ahead, with houses to the right. This quickly emerges into a field corner, where turn right on a pathless course outside the houses. After modern houses at the end advance to a stile onto an enclosed path, which runs a pleasanter course along this side valley. Further on you emerge to advance to a stone-slab footbridge on the stream, with modern housing just ahead. Across, rise a few yards to a stile on the right, from where rise with the fence on your left and along the field top. Part way on, a kissing-gate transfers you to its other side. At the end a stile puts you onto an enclosed grassy path the short way to drop right to a footbridge on a streamlet. Cross to the old rail underpass ahead, emerging to ascend a steep field. Through a stile at its top corner a fenced path runs on past allotments to a stile back onto Cliffe Lane.

Go left up the footway back into Gomersal's suburbia. After the large house of Bawson Cliffe on the left, take a short access road left. At the houses an enclosed path advances straight on, dropping outside a field onto an access road at Throstle Nest. Turn right, rising steadily to rejoin suburbia at Latham Lane alongside Gomersal Methodist Church. *Built as a Wesleyan Methodist Chapel in 1828, it boasts a fine bowed front.* Cross straight over and along West Lane's footway past Gomersal Hall grounds. Rejoining the A651 at the end, cross and go briefly right to meet your outward route. Go left a few strides along Scott Lane, but this time take a snicket on the left between houses, winding around to emerge via a kissing-gate into a large field. The path descends its side, and at the bottom a kissing-gate accesses the A652.

Cross and go left the short way to Oakwell Hall entrance at Nutter Lane. As the road swings right, keep left on a broad path left of the Countryside Centre car park. Remain on this beneath an embankment of the old railway of earlier acquaintance, slowly rising to join it and advance along it. Further on at a fork in more open surrounds, remain on your way curving right, and dropping gently into trees. Through these and over a streamlet it rises away to run on to merge alongside an old rail bridge. Either take the broad track right, or a nicer, parallel path just before it: this runs through a small garden to emerge at the tearoom alongside the hall.

LOWER CALDER VALLEY

Hilly rambling discovering landmarks amid rich woodland

START *Mirfield (SE 203197; WF14 8AN)*

DISTANCE $6^3/4$ *miles ($10^3/4$km)*

ORDNANCE SURVEY 1:25,000 MAP
Explorer 288 - Bradford & Huddersfield

ACCESS *Start from town centre junction of A644 and Station Road. Three-hour car park at top of Station Road, or roadside parking lower down, on route. Bus and train from surrounding towns.*

Mirfield is a small town set by the River Calder, with a section of the Calder & Hebble Navigation by-passing weirs on the river. Descend Station Road, over the canal, under the railway, and becoming Hopton New Road to bridge the River Calder at Hopton Bridge. This is Lower Hopton, with the Flowerpot pub to your right. Turn briefly left, then at a slight kink take a snicket on the right in front of a short stone terrace. Soon reaching a path junction, turn sharp left to emerge onto a rough access road. Turn a few strides right towards the last house, then left on another snicket between gardens to a stile into a field. The path heads away outside wooded Briery Bank. Reaching a stile into the trees, instead take the path bearing left across the field to a stile and footbridge on tiny Valance Beck. Across, the path rises between hedgerows, soon emerging at a kissing-gate to resume up the fieldside.

At the top another kissing-gate puts you onto an enclosed cart track. From a stile opposite, a path bears gently left across an arable field to a stile onto a hedgerowed footway. Turn right on this for a super stride, gently dropping to a fork just before trees. While the left branch goes through a stile, yours runs straight on into the trees of Gregory Spring. With a streamlet on the right, you almost at once pass an idyllic pond on the left where we watched a kingfisher. The path runs on through trees, and ignoring lesser branches, soon broadens to rise with a wall to a gate out. It turns right up the large sloping fieldside, remaining true to the wall enclosing the wood. A sustained pull on this good path eases out as the wood ends, and the enclosed cart track runs on to Liley Hall, part dating from the 17th century. Keep to the right of the buildings to emerge onto the B6118, with the Hare & Hounds pub just two minutes to the right. *Ahead is a sweeping new view west to Castle Hill backed by a high Pennine skyline that includes shapely Meltham Moor.*

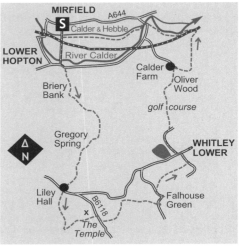

Cross and head away on a firm access road slanting down to the left. At a fork, ignore both and take a wall-stile on the left, from where a path slants across the field with the folly of The Temple up to your left. This runs on to an outer hedge corner and then along the hedgeside. Reaching a similar corner at the end, double back sharply left up the field. Rising towards trees, aim just 50 yards short of the end where a stile puts you onto a rough access road. *This was The Avenue that led to Whitley Beaumont Hall, demolished in the 1950s.* Cross to a stile into trees, and the path quickly ascends wooden steps into a clearing, with the folly a few yards off-route to your left. *Dating from around 1754 and known as Black Dick's Tower, its name recalls the supposed scoundrel Sir Richard Beaumont (1574-1631) of Whitley Hall: after selling his estate to clear gambling debts he became a highwayman, hence his nickname. its setting as a viewpoint is superb, and this knoll also marks the walk's high point at some 721ft/220m.*

The path resumes through a few trees and down a short field-side, then down through the wood back onto the B6118. Go briefly right on the footway, crossing to a grassy track descending between fields. When it quickly bears left, continue straight down a thinner but clear path. A little further, this is deflected left on an enclosed course between fields. Passing beneath the first power line, leave by a wall-stile on the right and head away along the hedgeside. *Emley Moor mast rises just across to the right.* At the bottom pass through successive gaps, then down an open field towards the next pylon. Before reaching it slant right down to the farm at Nickers Hill, using a stile onto its drive in front of the house. Drop left down the short drive onto a minor road at Falhouse Green.

Go left and ascend briefly to the house at Falhouse Farm, where the drive along the front leads to a gate at the end. A short enclosed way leads to a stile into a field. Through a gateway to the left, slant right up a rough pasture to find a stile in a kink at the top. Through it turn right along the hedgeside to a stile then gate at the end, then resume with the hedge on your left. Just ahead is Whitley Lower's church tower, and at the end bear left to the churchyard wall. Stiles outside it cross a small paddock, with a short snicket putting you onto Howroyd Lane alongside the church. *The sizeable church of St Mary & St Michael dates from 1847, with the old school house opposite.* Turn left past Church Farm the short way to a junction in Whitley Lower. *To your left is the Woolpack pub, with an ice cream parlour a little further up the road.*

The onward route turns right on Scopsley Lane along the top side of the pub, leaving housing behind and narrowing before a sharp bend right. Just a minute further, take a stile on the left onto Dewsbury & District golf course. Rise directly away on a distinct bank to a brow, then resume with it straight ahead to descend into a belt of trees. A clear path descends, soon down the side of the trees and through a further belt of trees. Emerging, drop straight down the last section of the course onto a track junction. Continue straight down, leaving the course with Oliver Wood on your right to drop down onto Sands Lane at housing at Calder Farm on your left.

Turn right on this, and as it swings right for Woodlands, keep straight on the continuing rougher lane. Shortly leave by a path on the left, whose double stone-flagged course briefly parallels the lane before swinging left to descend between fields into Lady Wood. The superb flagged surface maintains this direct descent, and only near the bottom do the flags abruptly end. Just a short way further the path arrives at a bridge over the railway. Cross and go left on the continuing parallel path, with the Calder just below. Soon bridging a sidestream, take a path bearing right to quickly drop down to merge with a riverbank path to head pleasantly upstream. Further, as the river swings away, the path runs through undergrowth the short way to emerge at the Ship Inn.

Turn right on the road over Shepley Bridge, then immediately left over a bridge on the canal, which at this point rejoins the river. This is the Shepley Bridge Cut of the Calder & Hebble Navigation: drop right onto the towpath at Shepley Bridge Lock. *Opposite are the old lock-keeper's cottage and a marina.* Head away along the towpath back to Station Road, en route passing Wheatley Bridge and Gill Bridge. Rise onto the road and re-cross to finish.

Black Dick's Tower

31

UNDER EMLEY MOOR

Two villages linked by old lanes, arable fields and a medieval industry in the shadow of a famous mast

START *Flockton (SE 240149; WF4 4DH)*

DISTANCE *6¹4 miles (10km)*

ORDNANCE SURVEY 1:25,000 MAP
Explorer 288 - Bradford & Huddersfield

ACCESS *Start from the village centre. Roadside parking, best on Pinfold Lane. Huddersfield-Wakefield bus.*

Flockton is a linear village spread along the busy A637 and hoping to one day be by-passed. At its eastern end is Jacks pub, and at its western end is a former Zion United Reformed Church of 1802. More centrally placed are St James the Great church, the Sun Inn and a Post office/shop. From the main road just east of the church, descend Pinfold Lane to the village edge. At the bottom, turn right immediately over the bridge onto a fieldside path outside the tree-lined stream. The path soon ends at the end of an access road, Common Lane. Continue on past some houses to a fork in front of a short terrace: the right branch goes up to the main road, the left branch is yours. Quickly losing its surface it leaves the houses behind and alongside farm buildings narrows to a bridleway. Its pleasant, dead-straight hedgerowed course rises ever gently to meet Haigh Lane at Six Lane Ends, with a short terrace opposite.

Don't join the road but go left on the broad, rough Crawshaw Lane, rising to a brow where it levels out and becomes pleasanter. At this high point of the walk the landmark mast is now at its closest to your right. *The mast at Emley Moor transmitting station is a 1084ft concrete structure that opened in 1971: its predecessor famously collapsed in 1969 under a weight of ice in adverse weather conditions.* The lane runs on to a crossroads near Upper Crawshaw Farm shortly after the first house. Go straight on, with Emley's church tower ahead. After starting a gentle descent, take a stile on the left into a cornfield. A good path heads away, dropping gently to an outer hedge corner, then down with the hedge to a path junction at a stile on the left (not quite as per map). Here turn sharp right on the next cross-field path to another outer corner, then on with the hedge dropping to a corner stile. From another in the dip just below, ascend a steeper pasture to a small gate in a crumbling wall beneath the churchyard. Ascending into the churchyard, go straight up past the church onto the road.

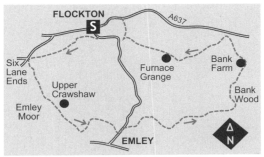

Best known for its nearby mast, Emley is a pleasant village with the church of St Michael the Archangel at its heart - note the old carvings incorporated into the wall by the war memorial. Also up to the right are the White Horse pub and a Post office/shop. An iconic white-painted cross at the junction is possibly a 13th century market cross, once bigger than it is now. Turn left a short way on Church Street, and just after the Methodist church turn right on Thorncliffe Lane. This quickly loses its surface and swings left to leave the houses and merges with one from the right. It runs on the short way to end at Thorncliffe Grange Farm. Advance straight through with barns and new houses on your right, with the early 17th century house itself set further back. Level with another house on your left, turn right before the last barn, crossing the small yard to the start of an enclosed, concrete path heading directly away. *As you get going look back right for a better glimpse of the house front's three gabled bays.* The path drops to a bend where it turns right and ends. From the left-hand of two gates a hedgeside path heads away, curving round to the left and rising marginally at a bend.

Pause at a stile on the right that drops precariously to a path junction. *The true right of way uses this to pass through a stile at an old gate on the left and along the pathless cornfield top, where successive stiles put you into a grassy pasture.* The preferred route however remains on the enclosed field-edge path to a gate at the end into a grassy pasture. *This vast field is the site of ancient iron workings, the subtle bumps and hollows of its pits having saved it from the plough. Iron ore was mined here when the area was administered from a grange of distant Byland Abbey on the edge of the North York Moors.* Drop right across it, crossing an early fence-stile and down to the far corner. Through the gate/stile descend the fieldside to a cross-paths at a stile below. Take the path straight ahead down the cornfield, quickly bearing right from the field edge to slant down to a stile in a tiny section of wall at the bottom. Just below, cross stepping-stones on Bank Wood Beck.

A path rises away through Bank Wood, quickly swinging left with a drain. It soon bridges this to ascend wooden steps pointing into a long, grassy clearing. Continue straight up back into trees, a steadier rise emerging onto a grassy cart track. Cross again for a gentle rise through trees, quickly reaching a wood-edge wall on your left. Just a little higher you leave the wood at a stile out into a cornfield, and a grassy hedgeside path heads away to Bank Farm. As the surfaced drive rises away, turn left on a briefly enclosed path past large barns immediately after a tiny pond. Advance on a fieldside to quickly veer right to run with a hedge on your left. When this swings right, pass through the gap and the path slants up across the cornfield to the A637 at Broad Oak Hill.

Without joining, double back left on a thin path commencing a gentle descent with the old boundary on your left. Before long the path bears right down the cornfield centre. *Ahead are Emley, its mast and Flockton.* The path slants down to a tree-lined streamlet on the other side, and down into trees at the bottom corner. Just below is a small footbridge on the stream, now known as Mill Beck. Emerging into an unkempt field with Furnace Grange ahead right, turn right on a poor path a short way from the stream. At an early bend locate a branch rising left through a rough patch, curving slightly left up and across to a hedge-stile in front. With relief cross and turn right with the hedge, over successive stiles to pass, briefly enclosed, beneath the house. *The farm is named from the area's history of iron workings, as already encountered.*

At the other end you enter a cornfield, and a good path heads away to a stile onto a descending access track. Continue straight across a briefly rougher section to the next stile, then an improved path runs a long, level course across to a footbridge and stile to rejoin the streamlet. Resume pleasantly with this around towards Millhouse Farm, the former Flockton Mill. From a stile to its right, follow the short drive out over a bridge, then double back right on the enclosed grassy way of Mill Lane. This quickly swings left for a pleasant rise to run along to join the main road in the village between houses. Go left on the roadside footway, passing en route a converted chapel of 1841 and the shop to return to the Pinfold Lane junction.

Emley church

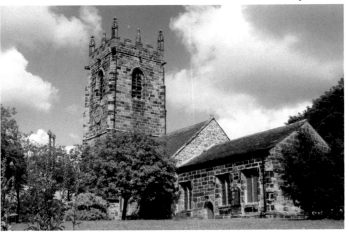

SCULPTURE PARK

A unique walking excursion through Yorkshire Sculpture Park

START *West Bretton (SE 287138; WF4 4LB)*

DISTANCE *5¼ miles (8½km)*

ORDNANCE SURVEY 1:25,000 MAP
Explorer 278 - Sheffield & Barnsley

ACCESS *Start from the village centre. Village hall car park off A637, honesty box. Wakefield-Barnsley bus. Dogs on leads in park, and not allowed in Upper Lake section (easily omitted).*

West Bretton village sits at the gateway to Bretton Country Park, an absorbing location for Yorkshire Sculpture Park. Rejoin the main road and turn right uphill, crossing to a footway opposite. Beyond Toll Bar Farm you gain the brow, and turn left on a cart track at the start of Wilderness Plantation. This runs a splendid course through the trees to ultimately reach a cross-tracks, where go sharp left. Briefly enclosed, you emerge via an old gateway into a parkland pasture, and a super path heads away. *Sweeping views look out over the upper Dearne Valley to a Pennine skyline featuring Black Hill.* The path curves gracefully down to a bridle-gate onto an access road at the edge of Bretton Park. *The park opened to the public in 1977, and an area of some 500 acres can now be explored. A regularly changing display of outdoor exhibits includes works by local superstars Henry Moore and Barbara Hepworth.*

Entering the park, either follow the driveway or preferably head straight down the grass, encountering Barbara Hepworth's 'The Family of Man' to drop down to the Rushbond Building (YSP Learning), with car park, café and WC. Continue straight down into 'Arcadia' in the Lower Park, passing more exhibits to reach a large open court with an enormous 'rabbit' sculpture outside the Camellia House dating from around 1812. Continue down the grass again onto a broader pathway, with the Lower Lake in view ahead.

Back up to the left is Bretton Hall itself. *The first documented house on the site was built for Sir Thomas Wentworth, Knight Marshall to Henry VIII. Damaged by fire in 1720, it was replaced by the present Hall in the 1730s for Sir William Wentworth. More recently, for around half a century until 1977, the house and ancillary buildings formed a campus of Leeds University, which after several derelict years is planned to become a hotel.* Turn right along the broader pathway to quickly reach a cross-paths with a

broad access track. Just to your left is a canal bridge, with Cascade Bridge immediately beyond it. *The old canal known as The Cut was created to carry water from the River Dearne, past the lakes to supply a blast furnace within the park.*

Go straight across to a gate into the wooded surrounds of the Upper Lake. A broad track heads away, while the more interesting right branch path rises slightly to pass the Summer House. *This early 19th century folly in the style of a Greek temple occupies a commanding position overlooking the Upper Lake.* Drop down past the Obelisk to rejoin the main way, which curves around to bridge the broad canal to the Boathouse. *This features six stone columns from the original building, dating possibly from as far back as the*

1760s: it stands landlocked in woodland due to silting up. Over the head of the lake the path swings left to return down the south bank. A footbridge crosses a small ravine, then a bird-hide sits just to the left. When the path forks, the left option visits the Shell Grotto. *Dating from the late 18th century, it retains old shells affixed to its interior, and gives further good views over the lake.* The paths rejoin to emerge onto the access road just above Cascade Bridge.

Turn right on the broad way rising to a gateway out of the park. As it climbs away, take the more inviting grassy left branch rising by a fence towards the Longside Gallery. *This delightful section through cattle-grazed grassland enjoys big views back to the hall.* At the top a bridle-gate puts you onto a firm path, going left the few yards to a fork. The right branch rises to the Longside Gallery with displays, café and WC. The onward route follows the broad, enclosed path running to diminutive Round Wood. Through a gateway the path rises past a circular stone structure to a gateway back out, then rises briefly onto the brow of Oxley Bank, going left to enjoy a magnificent stroll along its crest. *This finest stage of the walk overlooks the colourful bank as foreground to expansive views west.* This crest descends gently into more woodland. *On your right are Andy Goldsworthy's 'Hanging Trees', three box-like enclosures containing tree trunks.* Further you emerge at a field-side corner, and the path runs left over a ditch and wall to resume through Oxley Bank Wood. The '71 Steps' drop you down onto the

Lower Lake-side path: go right past Lady Eglington's Well to the dam end. Cross the embankment to bridge the canal as it turns to drop through cascades, and through a gate you re-enter the park.

   Turn right on the firm, grassy path running a level course to The Weston, featuring a gallery, restaurant and shop. Rejoin the hard track in front and rise away on it, bearing left across the park-land to pass through a fence gateway alongside stone sheepfolds: up to your left is a Henry Moore sculpture. As the path forks, bear right up into trees hiding St Bartholomew's chapel. *Designed by Sir William Wentworth in 1744, it now houses small exhibitions.* Re-emerging, its access track runs to a junction, where take the firm grass path slanting right towards the YSP Centre. An access road is crossed before reaching a small gate into the car park. *This hub of the park has full visitor facilities including shop and refreshments, as well as the Underground Gallery, exhibitions and some formal gardens.*

   To finish, double back right between the car park and the park fence to shadow the access road out, passing a final Henry Moore sculpture on the right. You also pass Archway Lodge of 1806 to a cattle-grid onto the A637 roundabout. Cross and go left on the footway the short distance back to the village centre. As you enter you pass the war memorial and 200-year old red-brick Manor House.

Opposite: The Chapel, Bretton Park   Emley Moor from Oxley Bank

THE CALDER & HEBBLE

Dead-flat walking by riverbank and towpath

START *Horbury Bridge (SE 280180; WF4 5NL)*

DISTANCE *5³⁄4 miles (9¹⁄4km)*

ORDNANCE SURVEY 1:25,000 MAP
Explorer 278 - Sheffield & Barnsley

ACCESS *Start from bridge on A642. Roadside parking
on Bridge Road and Old Bridge Road by café.
Bus from Dewsbury, Wakefield and Huddersfield.*

The settlement of Horbury Bridge stands outside the small
town of Horbury astride the River Calder, with the Calder &
Hebble Navigation running parallel. The substantial bridge is a
major crossing of the Calder. The adjacent Bingley Arms was
closed at the time of writing, though just across the road are a
popular café, the Horse & Jockey pub and a Post office/shop. The
Salvation Army's anthem 'Onward, Christian Soldiers' was written
here by local curate Sabine Baring-Gould in 1865. From the bridge
walk the very short way back towards the end of the first industrial
buildings. Here, before the road bends right, turn right along a
short-lived access road to further units. At the end an enclosed
path takes over, running between units and soon emerging close by
the river. Industry remains alongside for some time before you
enter an open area where a grassy embankment forms. This takes

40

the path along to arrive alongside a large pedestrian footbridge on the Calder. *This was built to carry a short mineral line from Hartley Bank Colliery on the opposite bank down to the main line.*

Ignoring the bridge, keep straight on the embankment which quickly ends at a derelict red-brick factory. Pass to its right to emerge via short-lived scrub into a fieldside. Simply remain on the riverbank path's pleasant course, partly into woodland and along to pass beneath a railway bridge. *This carried the Horbury West Curve, last used for freight in 1991.* Ignoring any branches left you arrive at another short embankment, again leading to a derelict red-brick factory. Again passing right, the path becomes enclosed between a fence and the river. A sizeable loop leads around to a path junction by a tiny red-brick ruin. Ignore an enclosed path left and keep on a short way further around a nice river bend towards the weir. Just before it the path leaves the river to emerge onto Millfield Road at an industrial estate at Horbury Junction.

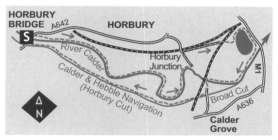

Go left on the footway, passing the Calder Vale pub and a former co-operative store of 1897 to a junction in front of a railway bridge. Turn right here on Forge Lane parallel with the line, leaving housing for an industrial site, where you cross several long-abandoned rail sidings. Under the railway bridge at the end you enter a rough car park: advance to a track at its other side which rapidly ends just short of the shore of Horbury Lagoon. *Previously Horbury Sailing Lake, this was originally an area of gravel pits.* Turn left on a lakeshore path which runs a pleasant course around to a corner beneath the M1 motorway, then beneath its embankment to the south-east corner. Here the path rises to a junction in front of the river again, alongside the motorway bridge.

Turn right for a nice stroll on the Calder's embankment path. When the embankment curves right, remain on the thinner but good riverbank path delving into undergrowth. Alternating between greenery and open stretches, it passes the easily missed Calder & Hebble rejoining the river at Broad Cut Bottom Lock. The path runs a splendid course along to a railway bridge, where you cross the river by way of an intriguing arrangement accessed by a few metal steps. The path runs an enclosed, illuminated course beneath the railway, dropping down more steps at the other end. Just to the left is the head of a short access road, with the popular canalside Navigation pub alongside Waller Bridge just in front.

Turn into the pub car park, where a small gate on the left puts you onto the towpath of the Horbury Cut of the Calder & Hebble Navigation. *Completed in 1770 to make the river navigable from the Aire & Calder Navigation at Wakefield west to Halifax and Sowerby Bridge, this section of waterway including the Horbury and Broad Cuts runs almost 6 miles west to Thornhill, avoiding weirs and bends on the river.* Turn right, passing beneath the busy Calder Grove railway bridge to Broad Cut Top Lock just ahead. The path now runs a splendid course through open countryside all the way back to the start. *Features include attractive woodland, a stretch of the river alongside, and several bridges.* Approaching Horbury Bridge a broad path slants right up past the Bingley Arms to the road: turn right to cross the bridge itself to finish.

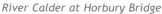

River Calder at Horbury Bridge

RIVER DEARNE

A lengthy streamside stroll beneath wooded Woolley Edge

START *Woolley (SE 320131; WF4 2JG)*

DISTANCE *5³4 miles (9¹4km)*

ORDNANCE SURVEY 1:25,000 MAP
Explorer 278 - Sheffield & Barnsley

ACCESS *Start from the village centre, roadside
parking. Infrequent Wakefield-Barnsley bus.*

Woolley is a small village set around a triangular green, and its core is a conservation area. St Peter's church boasts a solid tower and late medieval stained glass. The splendid Old Court House stands at a corner of the green, with other attractive buildings close by. Also facing the green is the village hall, occupying the former school of 1842. Woolley Hall on the village edge dates in part from 1635, and this long-time home of the Wentworth family is currently unoccupied. From the green turn right up High Street to a crossroads at a cenotaph garden, with the church just to your left. Go straight across up Mollyhurst Lane, which soon expires at the last house. A splendid hedgerowed green way takes over, rising imperceptibly to a gate into an arable field. A path continues up the left side, levelling out to reach the far end. From a hidden gap-stile in the very corner, a good path resumes the direction across an arable field to a stile onto Woolley Edge Lane.

Go right 40 yards and cross to a gap opposite, where a few steps atop Woolley Edge see a path with an old wall into Jobson Wood. *The gentle escarpment of Woolley Edge drops through wooded slopes to the west from the plateau on which the village stands.* The path drops slightly right then down to approach the wood edge. Ignoring a wall-stile in front, take a clear path left just yards earlier to run a pleasant, slanting course down through trees. Emerging at the end, advance on a pathless open field towards a scout camp. Approaching the building ahead, bear right through a line of trees to a gap in the hedge just below. From here a path descends an arable field to meet an access road at the bottom. From the stile just in front, descend a pasture to another stile (not the woodland shown on the map), and then down an unkempt fieldside towards Moorhouse Farm. Pass right of the buildings onto Moorhouse Lane, and turn right along it to emerge onto Haigh Lane.

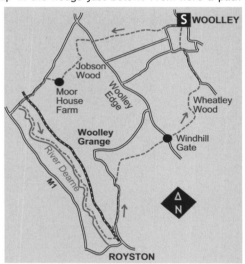

Cross over and follow a suburban footway down to pass under a railway bridge at the bottom, and on to approach a roundabout accessing the M1. Just before it, cross to a gate on the left immediately before the bridge over the River Dearne. A path heads away to commence a lengthy accompaniment of the meandering stream, alongside an arable field. Ignoring a footbridge, a nicer section tramps a slender strip of unkempt grassland, emerging to resume as before. Entering a wooded bank beneath a railway embankment, the path emerges into Longfields Community Green Space. A firm, made path immediately heads away, and can be followed the full length of this local green space, or alternatively you can stay true to the Dearne on a good stream-side path. Towards the end ignore another footbridge as the path becomes tarmac. *The map indicates non-existent woodland here, while Darton's solid church tower appears ahead.*

At the end bear left of a terrace of houses on the edge of Darton, joining an access road beneath the railway station. Go a couple of yards right and through the underpass, then left into the station car park. At its far right corner a tarmac path rises through greenery to quickly emerge onto Woolley Colliery Road. Go left on the broad footway opposite for a good few minutes to the major housing development of Woolley Grange. *This occupies the site of once extensive Woolley Colliery, which employed around 2000 men at its peak, but closed in 1987.* Simply remain on this road, new housing to your left contrasting with miners' terraces on your right.

The road narrows and rises to swing right through trees to end at a final house. Pass through the gate just beyond it into trees, and two paths head away. Take the right one to commence a gentle rise at Windhill Wood. *You are tracing the course of Wheatley Colliery Incline, a tramway that served a small mine on the hilltop ahead.* The trees quickly fade to leave a splendid hedgerowed way gently rising and broadening to emerge alongside houses onto Woolley Edge Lane at Windhill Gate. Cross straight over and along a rougher access road towards Beamshaw Farm. *The stables here occupy the site of modest Wheatley Wood Colliery.* At the gates the path runs an enclosed, parallel course to the left, passing the stables to a kissing-gate at a path junction. Pass through and follow the track left the short way to a gate into Wheatley Wood.

Take the left-hand, main track heading away into the trees. It remains close to the left edge, later swinging right to drop down, narrowing to leave the wood at old gateposts at the far corner. A short, enclosed continuation drops down a fieldside onto hedgerowed Woodhouse Lane. Go left for a few minutes back towards Woolley. At a T-junction on the village edge go briefly left, then turn into a short driveway on the right. On your right behind the house a wall-stile sends you across a grassy pasture, with the church just over to the left. Further on, ignore a gate on your right and continue on to the end, where a stile sends a snicket between gardens to emerge back onto the village green.

NEWMILLER DAM

Fine woodland and an old railway beyond a popular lake

START *Newmillerdam (SE 331157; WF2 6QQ)*

DISTANCE *7$\frac{1}{2}$ miles (12km) (with options to shorten)*

ORDNANCE SURVEY 1:25,000 MAP
Explorer 278 - Sheffield & Barnsley

ACCESS *Start from large Country Park car park alongside A61. Wakefield-Barnsley bus.*

Newmillerdam Country Park is a popular venue for gentle reservoir circuits, with assorted refreshment opportunities either side of the dam. The original, much smaller dam was built to serve a cornmill. From the car park entrance turn right on the footway across the embankment of Newmiller Dam. *Across the road are the Fox & Hounds pub and a cafe, while en route you pass 200-year old Sowtail Well and the West Lodge, now a restaurant, At the far end are the Dam Inn, cafe, WC and war memorial.* Over the dam turn right on the path past the East Lodge for a steady stroll along the reservoir's wooded shore to soon arrive at the Boathouse. *This attractive early 19th century structure of the Pilkington family serves refreshments on Summer Sundays.*

The path continues on to reach a concrete causeway. *This very pleasant spot offers the ultimate short-cut.* Resume to soon reach a major fork past the head of the lake. The right branch runs to a bridge across the stream, while your way is straight ahead to rise gently through trees. This soon arrives a level bridleway, where bear right to resume through the woods. Ignore a lesser right fork, and just ahead is a major cross-paths: keep straight on to run to a kissing-gate out of the trees. A good path continues across an arable field, soon merging with the tree-lined streamlet. Cross on a tiny stone-arched bridge, and ignoring a broad path rising away, resume upstream on a good path. Before long this is signed right up another broad ascending path between crops to enter the trees above. *In the deep cutting in front is the old Chevet branch line, which principally carried freight between 1909 and 1968.*

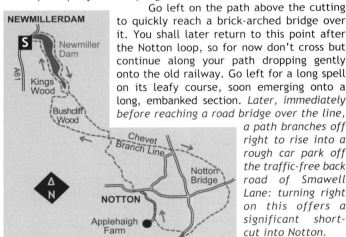

Go left on the path above the cutting to quickly reach a brick-arched bridge over it. You shall later return to this point after the Notton loop, so for now don't cross but continue along your path dropping gently onto the old railway. Go left for a long spell on its leafy course, soon emerging onto a long, embanked section. *Later, immediately before reaching a road bridge over the line, a path branches off right to rise into a rough car park off the traffic-free back road of Smawell Lane: turning right on this offers a significant short-cut into Notton.*

Remain on the railway under the B6132 bridge and on beneath another tall arched bridge to curve around to approach another stone-arched road bridge. Don't pass under this but bear right up a short, stepped path onto a road. Cross straight over and along an enclosed path parallel with the old line down to your left. Quickly approaching woodland, take the lesser right branch through a gap to resume along the field edge outside trees. Curving round a corner it leads to a clump of trees alongside a stone bridge over another former rail branch. Across this, turn sharp right to run a field-edge course overlooking the deep hollow of the overgrown line. At the end your path improves to run a broad, hedgerowed course out onto a road junction on the edge of Royston. *This is the site of the former Notton for Royston Station, located plum on the boundary with South Yorkshire.*

Bear right, and immediately past the old rail bridge site, turn sharp left on a firm path beneath the line. As Green Lane this bears right to run a splendid, enclosed course through a gentle hollow to emerge onto Applehaigh Lane. Turn right on the footway alongside Applehaigh Wood for a few minutes into Notton. *This largely modern village is based around an extensive, triangular green overlooked by a Post office/shop.* Advance past the shop then left on the through road, briefly, before crossing to turn right along the suburban street of Ingswell Drive. At an immediate fork go right a few yards, then left along a snicket between houses. Emerging into a field corner, the firm path runs straight on outside gardens on your left, and as suburbia terminates you cross a footbridge into open fields. Remain on the main, broad path heading away, now commencing a splendid, very gently rising stride on a broad green way through arable fields. It bends left and then right, along the crest of the field to trees ahead where you find the old bridge on the cutting from earlier.

Cross and retrace steps a few yards to the left, then take a stepped path down onto the line. Turn right to commence a lengthy spell back to the country park, the cutting soon replaced by a long embankment. On approaching Bushcliff Wood and a tall three-arched bridge, take a path bearing right to rise to the bridge end. Don't cross, but turn right a few strides to a path junction in the trees. Go left the short way onto a minor brow, where a thinner but clear path forks right. Follow this down through the trees, over a cross-track and down to run along to rejoin the now level main track. Ignore the thinner continuation and bear right on the broad way to run a level course, soon winding down onto a broader junction at a clearing. Go left the few yards to an open area by the reservoir-head bridge from early in the walk. Again don't cross but turn left on the firm, broad path. Within a minute the lake appears, and ignore any branches left as you initially trace a drain. The lake soon opens out and remains alongside all the way back to the start.

Barnsley Canal

Easy strolling by woodland, towpath, lake and reservoir

START *Wintersett (SE 374153; WF4 2EB)*

DISTANCE *5³⁄₄ miles (9¹⁄₄km)*

ORDNANCE SURVEY 1:25,000 MAP
Explorer 278 - Sheffield & Barnsley

ACCESS *Start from Anglers Country Park car park at Waterton Countryside Discovery Centre signed on Haw Park Lane.*

Anglers Country Park occupies what was claimed as the country's deepest open-cast coalmine at some 250 feet: it closed in 1982. The soulless yet soothing lake sits amid a reinvigorated landscape, popular with wintering waterfowl. The visitor centre has a tea-room and WC. Rejoin Haw Park Lane and turn right past a sailing club on Cold Hiendley Reservoir. Remain on this all the way, losing its surface after it trades woodland for fields to approach Haw Park Wood. Within a minute of entering, a major junction is reached, where take a firm track sharp left. *In the 1600s this was part of the ancient Don Forest, largely felled to make way for agriculture. The mid-20th century saw much ancient woodland planted over to produce timber and pit props for local coal mines, but the wood is being returned to a deciduous scene from its pines and larches.*

At an early fork keep left along the wood edge, soon swinging right to drop gently through the trees. When the track swings sharp right at the bottom, continue straight down a less firm, still broad path. Passing Fox's Well the path drops to a corner junction in front of the drained Barnsley Canal. *Completed in 1802 principally to carry coal north from Barnsley, it ran for some 15 miles to Heath Common on the outskirts of Wakefield, linking with the Aire & Calder Navigation. Abandoned in 1947, it closed in 1953 after a major leak flooded housing: only limited sections still carry water.* Turn left to leave the wood corner, and advance a few strides over the bridge of the outflow of Cold Hiendley Reservoir to appraise an attractive scene. *Built in 1854 to supply the canal, it was enlarged 20 years later.*

Re-entering the wood, bear immediately left on a firm, broad path to the left of the drained canal. This runs a pleasant, easy course in close company with the canal, quickly passing a stone-arched bridge. Further, the canal becomes part

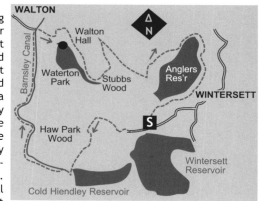

watery, and this route is maintained to reach Clay Royd Bridge at the wood end. Don't cross but simply continue for some time still, with open fields to your left. Passing beneath a tall-arched bridge in a deep rocky cutting, remain on the towpath to ultimately arrive at a fork just short of a stone-arched bridge. Bear left here up onto the road at the bridge side, with a large golf clubhouse ahead. Turn right over the bridge and along the access road through the golf course: it serves Walton Hall, which soon appears ahead. *Dating from 1767, the large house occupies an island on a lake, and now operates as the Waterton Park Hotel. It is best known as the home of Charles Waterton (1782-1865), a pioneering naturalist who brought species back from South America's tropical forests, and in 1813 created what was deemed the world's first nature reserve.*

Dropping down, look out for a path branching left immediately at the start of woodland. This briefly traces the wood edge before delving into the trees, going left a few yards with a brick wall and through a gateway in it. It then drops through scrub and down a fenceside to emerge onto an unsurfaced access road. Go briefly right to emerge back at the golf course, and as it rises into the open, instead take a path right along the front of a garage. This rises gently through scrub and scattered woodland, soon reaching a waymarked grassy fork. Bear right, but within yards at an unmarked fork with a car park just ahead, bear left on a thinner path through grass. This quickly crosses rough grassland back to a cross-tracks with a golfers' track: go straight across on a track along the base of a wooded bank. Much of the lake is now in view, and the hall returns to view back to your right as you rise gently to an old tee at a junction.

Take the inviting path straight ahead, quickly delving into Stubbs Wood and finally leaving the course. Ignoring an early left branch, remain on this splendid woodland path, dropping gently to approach the water's edge at the head of the lake. Here the path swings left and resumes, ignoring a cross-path and continuing past a sizeable pond outside the woodland boundary. At a short length of forlorn wall on your right the path leaves the trees and runs along an old boundary, with the golf course again just up to your left. The path runs nicely on alongside and then through shrubbery to reach another section of wall at a path junction. Here double back sharply right, a path descending an arable field to the bottom, where a boardwalk leads the short way along to successive kissing-gates. The path rises up a hedgeside and along two fieldsides to a kissing-gate at a bend, putting you onto the broad, firm, enclosed path encircling the as yet unseen Anglers Country Park Reservoir. *For a quicker finish go right here.*

Turn left for some ten minutes until reaching a branch right. This more regular but still firm path runs a short way through trees to emerge into a grassy area by the reservoir shore. Go left, and a little further the other branch comes back in. All is now entirely open as the firm path leads back towards the visitor centre. *Near the end, a signed path offers a short diversion left into Wintersett village to visit the Anglers Retreat pub.* At the reservoir end keep left on the main track the short way back to the start.

THE AIRE & CALDER

A lengthy towpath stroll from a fascinating old village

START Heath (SE 356198; WF1 5SL)

DISTANCE 7 miles (11¼km)

ORDNANCE SURVEY 1:25,000 MAP
Explorer 278 - Sheffield & Barnsley
Explorer 289 - Leeds

ACCESS Start from the village centre, car park on green. Wakefield-Castleford bus.

Heath is a splendid village close by busy roads just outside of Wakefield, with extensive commons to the south and spacious greens at the centre. Focal point is the Kings Arms, a superb old multi-roomed pub lit by gas lamps. The entire village is a time-warp, with almost every building being of architectural merit. Just south of the car park are a restored pinfold and the Whittling Well. Facing the pub, go left and through a narrow open area onto a spacious green, and head north along this to the far corner. *On your right are the Dower House of 1740 and imposing Heath Hall, dating from 1709 and extended later that century by John Carr for John Smyth.* At the end you join Kirkthorpe Lane leaving the village.

A footway leads along outside the weathered old wall of the hall grounds, soon reaching a lay-by where an enclosed path drops left into trees at the Ashfields. Reaching a junction, you shall return by the right-hand path. *You are entering the Southern Washlands, a series of linked nature reserves on old coal mining sites or former sand and gravel pits.* Go left on the broad path through a gateway down to a junction in a dip in the trees. Just a few yards up the other side is a second junction: turn right on a broad, embanked path. Towards the end drop right at a fork to pass beneath a railway arch. Emerging, the path runs a straight course enclosed in greenery to reach Blue Bridge, a massive metal foot-bridge over the River Calder. To your left is Broad Reach Lock at the start of a section of the Aire & Calder Navigation.

This major canal was completed in 1704 in order to make the River Aire navigable as far as Leeds, and increasing demand on this busy waterway saw new locks and cuts added in the 19th century. At one time all manner of produce was shipped in from Goole and Hull docks to Leeds, and much coal shipped out the other way. To this day you might still see commercial traffic carrying the likes of sand and oil. The canal was once known for its 'Tom Puddings', a string of smaller craft pushed by a tug.

Across, the firm, stony way of the Trans-Pennine Trail heads off through undergrowth, but it's nicer to take a grassy path doubling back left 100 yards through bracken to the lock. *As with all canal sections, young children need supervision.*

Turn right on the grassy towpath, quickly rising to pass alongside an early bridge. The firmer cycle path runs parallel to the right, but preferably drop back to the towpath for a lovely stroll on grass as far as the next bridge, Harrisons Bridge. Keep straight on to find an access road dropping to the towpath, its grassy verge offering a pleasant stride along its dead-straight course, passing countless barges on the approach to Stanley Ferry Moorings. At Ramsdens

Bridge a swing bridge and tall footbridge give the option to visit the Stanley Ferry pub by the water's edge just ahead. On your bank, meanwhile, you quickly arrive at the red-brick terrace of Aire & Calder Cottages, with a marina by the pub opposite.

Passing left of the houses you arrive at Stanley Ferry aqueduct, two parallel bridges over the River Calder. *The celebrated cast iron arched structure of 1839 was a magnificent engineering feat of its time, though basically replaced in 1981 by its soulless concrete counterpart alongside.* A third bridge, the Trash Screen Bridge, carries you over the tree-lined river, rejoining the towpath at a grassy area opposite workshops where lock gates are made. *Stanley Ferry takes its name from the original river crossing upstream, which was replaced by a toll bridge, itself replaced by the present road bridge in 1971.* Leaving this colourful scene behind, pass under Altofts Bridge to resume in open countryside, swinging around to Birkwood Bridge and Lock. Here an access road leads on the remaining part of your towpath trod.

The point to leave comes at the end of a field beyond a clump of trees. A stile and waymark send you away along the hedgeside of an arable field, through a stile and on to the corner where the way turns right. The path in this short section is poor, indeed from the corner it was noted that previous walkers had opted to trace a tractor track a short way out from the hedge. As the hedge turns sharp left, a stile on the near side of the corner sends a better hedgeside path away to a stile/gate onto a track. This slants right between horse pastures up to a gate at the top, where it runs an enclosed course to Top Farm. Noting the fine red-brick barn in the yard, take a gate on the right, and adjacent stiles put you onto a road on the edge of Altofts.

Cross straight over to an enclosed, flagged bridleway heading away to soon emerge into an open cornfield. This runs a splendid course featuring another short section of causey part way on. At the end it continues alongside a wood, dropping at the end onto a rough access road. Go right a few strides and resume on another firm path, through a cornfield then dropping down into a vast open area of reclaimed coal workings. At the bottom cross over a path and, with Newland Lakes on your right, keep straight on to a signed path junction. Go straight ahead through a stile into trees, and immediately take the right fork to run beneath a wooded bank.

Just after a glimpse of the adjacent lake comes a fork: go left, and almost at once fork left again on a thinner but clear path into scrub. This meanders along to a small clearing by a tall fence on your left. Keep straight on into woodland to quickly drop to a broader, firmer path. Go left above the River Calder, immediately under a concrete colliery bridge. This runs a largely excellent course with intermittent river views, and passing a pond on the left. Just after a path comes in from the left, the path veers left to slant up to an access road. Cross straight over to resume beneath a tall railway bridge, then slant right up out of the trees, now as a firmer way. This runs to a gate at an access road-end by houses at Kirkthorpe. Follow this drive the short way out to Half Moon Lane in the hamlet, passing the church on your left. *With its solid 14th century tower, St Peter's occupies a peaceful setting.*

Joining Half Moon Lane, just to your left is Frieston's Hospital, almshouses founded in 1595 by John Frieston of Altofts and now a private dwelling. Drop right a few strides and go left on a pathway running into trees, and tramping a nice course with Half Moon Pond glimpsed below. *This former meander of the Calder was cut adrift by construction of the railway line in 1838.* Ignoring branches right the path soon runs on to the junction near the start. Rise left and return on the roadside footway into Heath.

The old path back from Altofts

FAIRBURN INGS

*A pair of fascinating villages linked by old paths add
great interest to the highlight of a major nature reserve*

START *Fairburn (SE 451277; WF10 2BH)*

DISTANCE *5 miles (8km)*

ORDNANCE SURVEY 1:25,000 MAP
Explorer 289 - Leeds

ACCESS *Start from RSPB visitor centre on Newton Lane a mile
west of village. Both Fairburn and Ledsham have bus services.*

Fairburn Ings is a flagship reserve of the Royal Society for the
Protection of Birds. Originally an extensive area of wetlands and
marshes, 20th century coal mining brought about flooding which
ultimately was put to good use as a large lake was created, now
renowned for its wildfowl. In 2017, spoonbills nested here for the
first time in 400 years in Yorkshire. From the car park entrance
cross the road to an informal path heading away across open
ground to join a minor road. Directly opposite, a broad path heads
away along the edge of Newfield Plantation. *This historic way of
Newfield Lane leads all the way to Ledsham, though today is
largely no more than a footpath.* Ignoring branches into the trees,
it levels out to run a super course with open fields to your right. At
the wood end, continue along a field boundary the short way to
resume with another wood dropping away to your left. At the end

a gentle rise reveals the church spire at Ledsham ahead, and the path runs on alongside an old field boundary. Broadening into a cart track at the end, it emerges onto the head of a short access road which leads out onto the village street.

Ledsham is a truly delightful village, close by the Great North Road and also the very easternmost parish of Leeds District, yet feels a million miles away from either motorway or city. Its street winds timelessly around from the historic Chequers Inn to All Saints church, fronted by an old pump and stone trough. The church

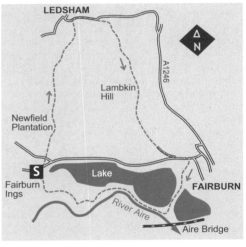

is *especially ancient and beautiful: a spire crowns the Norman tower of Saxon origin, incorporating a restored Saxon doorway at its base. Other historic parts abound, and with 15th century work it later suffered Victorian restoration. Inside is a resplendent memorial of Sir John Lewis and his wife of nearby Ledston Hall. Behind the church a private path leads to view the lovely row of Sir John Lewis's Cottages, almshouses he founded in 1670. Alongside the church is the attractive, three-storey Lady Betty Hastings' Orphanage of 1721, founded by Lady Elizabeth Hastings, grand-daughter of Sir John.*

Turn right on the neat footway which expires at the old school, with its bell still in situ. A short way further, after the last house and at the village sign, a gate set back on the right at a lay-by sends an inviting path away alongside scattered trees on your right. This soon swings right through a gateway and resumes beneath trees into the base of Wormstall Wood. Ignore the early fork left, and advance the short way to a stile out of the trees. Resume along a slender enclosure, and when the wood ends continue with the hedge on your right. Part way along the field ignore a left fork slanting up it, and keep on to short-cut the far corner to a stile ahead. The path crosses a belt of woodland and heads thinly away across an unkempt pasture. It rises gently left to broaden before gaining a path junction by a fence on the brow of Lambkin Hill.

Bear right on this super stroll along the bank top with open views. At the end pass through a kissing-gate, with a view down over the large lake at Fairburn Ings. Resume along a field edge above the wooded bank of Caudle Hill Plantation, and after a further kissing-gate the path becomes enclosed as it leaves the bank top. Running on to join a driveway alongside a house, this runs on through trees to meet the access road of Beckfield Lane, which continues on to join Water Lane on the edge of Fairburn. Cross and bear left on the suburban footway to a broad junction with parking area and information panel at Welltrough Cottages.

Fairburn was once a busy village upon the Great North Road, and a heritage trail explores its many interesting features. The horse trough and pump stand at this very junction, while easily viewed just yards along the street is a former jail. There are two

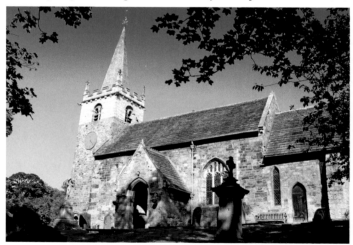

pubs, the Wagon & Horses and Three Horse Shoes. An enterprising underground railway was built in 1823 to run beneath the village from limestone and gypsum quarries to a canal (the Fairburn Cut) linking to the nearby River Aire for onward transportation. This survived for almost a century, and the stone spindle of the brake-wheel around which the incline cable ran now stands cross-like at a junction just past the jail.

Turn right past the pump down Cut Lane, quickly becoming a broad, firm pathway dropping onto the flatlands of Fairburn Ings. It runs a dead-straight, level course with the lake on your right and Fairburn Cut on your left. Crossing a bridge towards the end, you reach a path junction in front of the River Aire, with the rail viaduct of Aire Bridge to your left. Turn right to enter the reserve, a firm path initially rising slightly through trees along a distinct raised embankment. *Occasional glimpses of the river down to your left are bettered by glimpses of the lake.* Village Bay viewpoint is passed, and further, the Bob Dickins Hide. The lake ends here and the path soon winds up through a more open, scrubby landscape amid evidence of its coal mining past. The path finally crosses a brow to reveal a large hollow in front, and you drop onto a broader path. Turn right on this to enter more wooded surrounds, quickly arriving at a kingfisher hide on a drain. The path swings left here, and soon turn right onto a raised walkway across reedbeds to reach a path junction with the visitor centre just yards to your right.

Opposite: Ledsham church   *Fairburn Ings*

TEMPLE NEWSAM

Much of interest around a great country estate

START *Temple Newsam (SE 357321; LS15 0AE)*

DISTANCE *5^{1}4 miles (8^{1}2km)*

ORDNANCE SURVEY 1:25,000 MAP
Explorer 289 - Leeds

ACCESS *Start from Temple Newsam, signed along Colton Road off A63 at Whitkirk. Of several car parks, only that adjacent to the house has charges. Colton is served by bus from Leeds.*

Temple Newsam is an imposing Jacobean mansion set within well-wooded parkland. Its origins date back to a preceptory of the Knights Templar, medieval mercenaries. Most of the enormous red-brick house dates from the 1630s: for 300 years it was home to the Ingrams until acquired by Leeds Corporation in 1922. Its remarkable array of contents displayed within around 30 rooms includes a nationally important art collection. Externally its south front looks out over charming hedged gardens, while set around the 1788 skyline balustrades of its eastern courtyard are these words: ALL GLORY AND PRAISE BE GIVEN TO GOD THE FATHER THE SON AND HOLY GHOST ON HIGH PEACE EARTH GOOD WILL TOWARDS MEN HONOUR TRUE ALLEGIANCE TO OUR GRACIOUS KING LOVING AFFECTION AMONGST HIS SUBJECTS HEALTH AND PLENTY BE WITHIN THIS HOUSE.

To the east of the house an 18th century stable block houses a visitor centre, exhibition rooms, estate shop, tearoom and WC. Adjacent Home Farm has been transformed with a successful rare breeds programme featuring cattle, sheep, goats and pigs, and also has a 300-year old Great Barn. Set just above the Menagerie Ponds is the beautiful red-brick Walled Garden, at the centre of which is an extensive rose garden. Both the house and the farm have entry fees. The extensive, rolling parkland was designed by Capability Brown in the 1760s. Just outside the grounds at the road entrance, the lovely St Mary's church at Whitkirk contains fine effigies.

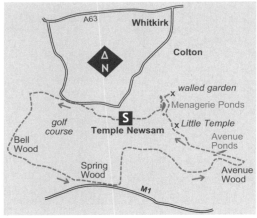

From the house entrance take a path to its right side, running alongside the house and continuing directly away by a grassy area, with the main car park to your right. Advance straight on into trees ahead, the broad footpath soon swinging to the right and narrowing: as it curves further right take a narrower branch path left over a tiny bank to advance the short way across grass to a hard path parallel with the estate road just ahead. Go left on the path to quickly join the road, now descending on a tree-lined roadside footway alongside a golf course. As the road swings right, continue straight down a firm track across the course, at the bottom entering trees. Just up the other side bear left at a fork, rising and quickly levelling to cross the course and along to another junction with open views across a new wood.

Here go left on the broad, firm path descending between the golf course and Bell Wood, soon into more woodland. This remains unchanged for some time, with the course always close by. At the end swing sharp left on the main path when a lesser branch goes right into the open. This continues again for some time through Bell Wood, later along the wood edge with open grassland to your right. At the end you emerge onto a tarmac lane that is merely a bridleway, with the M1 alongside. *This was the original Pontefract Lane before the motorway intervened. The fringes of the grounds were exploited for coal until quite recent times.*

Go left, rising above the parallel motorway to drop to a junction alongside an underpass. Swing left here on the tarmac bridleway which soon ascends through trees to approach an angled cross-ways on a grassy brow. Here, at Dunstan Hills with a glimpse of the house ahead, turn right across the grass. Cross a firm track onto a more inviting, tall-hedgerowed green way heading directly away. This contrastingly grassy delight soon drops markedly to a gate onto another stony track. Go right just a few paces and take a bridle-gate on the left into woodland. A small path runs through, bridging a streamlet to another small gate back out onto a cart track.

Cross straight over to an enclosed path rising into greenery, soon easing out to cross a wooden footbridge over the parallel streamlet. Resume on the other side, ignoring a right branch and running grandly on to rise briefly onto a path along the wood top. Go left, rapidly back into woodland where drop left a few yards on a woodside path to another fork. Bear right on a thinner path's short, level course to meet another path just above Avenue Ponds down to your left. Turn right up this through Avenue Wood, another good path that soon eases amid modest clearings, levelling out to swing left onto the broad path of The Avenue. Turn left on its dead-straight course with broad green verges, immediately revealing the mansion itself straight ahead. Dropping to bridge Avenue Ponds, it rises to a brow revealing the house again. As you drop away, keep to the track slanting right, down through trees to meet the bend of a firm access road. Through the gap-stile opposite, a path climbs by trees to a stile accessing the Little Temple. *Awaiting restoration, this occupies a knoll with a view across to the mansion.*

Resume along the firmer path to another stile into greenery, and the path slants gently down through rhododendrons, ignoring any lesser branches. Glimpsing the Menagerie Lakes to your left as you meet a level path, go right on this to quickly reveal more of the main lake. The path runs on to a junction towards the end, where drop left onto green spaces along the shore. Though your onward route is over the wooden footbridge just ahead, a very short detour advances a little further before going right up steps onto an access road with a WC to your left. Through the gates in front is the Walled Garden. Back at the footbridge, cross and bear left on the broad tarmac path. This swings away from the lake and rises alongside a hedge up the side of parkland, then climbing between rhododendrons to a path junction with the mansion just ahead. Continue straight up past the farm park and Stable Yard just short of the mansion.

Temple Newsam from The Avenue

St Aidan's

Easy walking at a wildlife haven reclaimed from industry

START *Allerton Bywater (SE 399287; LS29 8AL)*

DISTANCE *5$\frac{1}{2}$ miles (8$\frac{3}{4}$km)*

ORDNANCE SURVEY 1:25,000 MAP
Explorer 289 - Leeds

ACCESS *Start from RSPB St Aidan's nature reserve on Astley Lane at Great Preston, west of village. Castleford-Leeds bus.*

Allerton Bywater is a former coal mining community spread along the north bank of the Aire above Castleford. It is one of many such communities to have suffered the demise of coal: over a thousand men worked at its colliery only a year or so before its 1992 closure. St Aidan's reserve is managed by the RSPB for Leeds City Council on the very site of Allerton Main Collieries. An iconic, monumental 1200 tonnes dragline excavator dominates the visitor centre with refreshments and WC. Along with extensive lakes are restored reedbeds where you might hear the 'boom' of bitterns.

Pass between the centre and the 'digger' on a broad, firm path dropping away towards the reserve. Remain on this main way over a major cross-paths beneath a grassy bank, and with the start of reedbeds on your left you shortly reach the first lake, Fleakingley Reservoir on your right. A little further is a staggered junction: ignore both the left branch into the heart of the reedbeds, and the imminent stony right branch. Instead simply remain on the broader but nicer track ahead, with reedbeds on your left and a broad drain on your right. Quickly swinging sharp left, this is a splendid section. Ultimately Lemonroyd Lake forms on your right and you reach a major cross-paths. Turn right over the Causeway between the main lake and Lemonroyd Lake, at the end of which you reach another cross-paths at the edge of the reserve.

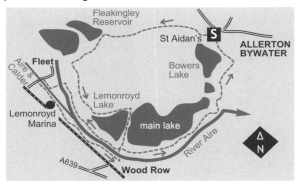

Through a gateway just ahead is another cross-paths in front of substantial Shan House Bridge on the River Aire. *Note that you could use a broader path right within the reserve boundary as far as a path signed left up the bank to a gateway for Lemonroyd Bridge, rejoining the main route there.* Pass out of the reserve but don't cross the river (you'll return this way after the Lemonroyd loop). Instead turn right on the firm, narrower path upstream between river and reserve fence. Scrub and woodland largely hide the Aire, though a later section offers a break at a small sandy beach. Further, you arrive alongside Lemonroyd Bridge on your left, with a reserve gateway on your right.

This time cross the river and advance the few strides to the Aire & Calder Navigation at Fleet. *For more on this major canal see WALK 13.* Turn right with the access road the short way to a road at Fleet Bridge, across which double back on the other bank. As the access road swings right for Lemonroyd Marina, cross a footbridge over the marina entrance to a pleasant area alongside Lemonroyd Lock. Beneath this massive lock the canal ends as the Aire returns.

Beneath the lock a path bears right into trees to merge with another broad path, resuming downstream through scrub and woodland. Within a minute branch left through a gate onto a path rising gently and running on, again with only occasional glimpses of the Aire until you arrive at Shan House Bridge. Re-cross the broad river amid total greenery and go straight ahead through the gateway back into the reserve. Turn right on the broad, stony track through scrub, quickly ending at a viewing platform for the main lake. Its place is taken by a contrastingly splendid grassy path, which runs along a modest embankment through open country. *On the reserve boundary, this enjoys spacious views over the lake.*

Eventually arriving alongside a bridleway at Caroline Bridge on the Aire, don't cross but remain on your path slanting down across a scrubby bank. A little further you are forced up onto the bridleway at a bridge over the lake outflow, with the river just to the right. Remain on the broad path at a junction just ahead where keep left, the path running near the small lake of Halfpenny Pool. A little further ignore a branch right, and go left a few yards to join Bowers Lakeside path running right to approach the visitor centre up the slope ahead.

The excavator at St Aidan's

BECCA BANKS

An ancient earthwork in the shadow of the Great North Road

START *Aberford (SE 433374; LS25 3AA)*

DISTANCE *5¹4 miles (8¹2km)*

ORDNANCE SURVEY 1:25,000 MAP
Explorer 289 - Leeds

ACCESS *Start from main street in vicinity of bridge, roadside parking. Bus from Leeds, Wetherby and Wakefield.*

Aberford is a classic street village a full mile in length, once a major coaching halt along the old Great North Road, though long since by-passed. It ceased to be a market town around 1800, and the Swan Hotel survived until 2014 as an old coaching inn. The uniquely named Arabian Horse pub stands back from an attractive, sloping triangular green. Aberford stands on the Cock Beck, which meanders for several miles to join the Wharfe near Tadcaster. A renovated watermill stands at the southern end of the long bridge. The church of St Ricarius is the only one in England so dedicated, recalling a 7th century French missionary: restored in the 19th century, its tower has Norman origins. Outside stands an old market cross on circular steps. Aberford's most remarkable feature is its incredibly ornate former almshouses, isolated at the southern end of the village: dating from 1844, they were built as a memorial by members of the Gascoigne family.

From the road bridge walk north along the street the short way to the Arabian Horse, opposite which head off along surfaced Becca Lane. It rapidly leaves the village behind to reach a wood on the left. Quickly escape the lane on a permissive path delving into the trees to run a delightful, level course, at once observing the earthwork of Becca Banks on your right. *Evident at regular intervals (even from the lane) is this distinct embankment just inside the trees, with the bank towering above a deep trench. Part of an ancient earthwork stretching for around three miles in an arc to the north of Aberford, it is an Iron Age defensive fortification of the Brigantes.*

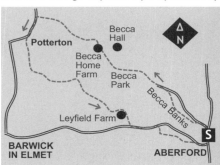

Your path soon arrives beneath the substantial Magnesian limestone cliff of Becca Banks Crag. *This runs for some 300 yards above the path, attracting occasional rock climbers.* Beyond, the path slants right back up onto the lane. Resume left the short way to a fork where it loses its surface: keep straight on (left) with the wood to reach a lodge. *Here the grand house of Becca Hall, dating from 1783, appears across the fields of Becca Park.* The drive heads across the fields towards the house, but after a small thrust of Becca Low Wood, leave it as directed by bearing left on a faint way across the parkland. Continue past the wood end and along to a corner gate at the far end. Turn right on a cart track, soon enclosed by hedgerows to reach Becca Home Farm.

Ignore the access road right and keep straight on the track ahead, but just 25 yards after a gate out of the yard by the last barn, turn off left down the field. If the crop is at full height, then the next five minutes can be trying. Ideally you might trace a trackway down, kinking left then down towards a waymark by a clump of trees. Go left for no more than fifty yards with the line of trees and streamlet, then turn right up the sloping field centre. An improved path rises in a direct line past an isolated tree, up to an outer edge of South Plantation. Continue straight on with the wood on your left, and remain on the fieldside path to a stile at the end. The path crosses this slender belt of trees to the next field, and then again runs along its left side outside Old Plantation. After dropping to a gateway, a thin trod slants right across a small field to a corner stile in the hedge. Joining the back road of Potterton Lane, go left to a sharp bend at the hamlet of Potterton.

A lodge on the left sits by the driveway to Potterton Hall, while your route is through a gate between houses straight ahead. As Grassy Miry Lane it now runs a delectable course between hedgerows. *Though only glimpsed through a gate at the start, parkland on the left is the site of the medieval village of Potterton. Not easily discerned, the earthworks, no more than grassy mounds, include house platforms and strips of ridge and furrow ploughing.* After the track makes a major turn left, the church tower at Barwick in Elmet rises out of the trees across fields to the right. The hedgerows end arbitrarily but the track continues, dropping to a gateway at the bottom and turning right with a hedge. Approaching a wood corner, keep straight on alongside Ridge Plantation. Ignore a first gap and continue to a corner where the track remains outside the trees. This time bear right through another gap with a distinct earthwork. *This splendid tall bank and deep ditch is The Ridge, a continuation of Becca Banks.*

Your route continues as a grassy path with trees on the right, dropping to swing left at a corner. Very quickly it turns right through greenery with an almost hidden pond on your left. A short way further through scrub you reach a bridle-gate after a stream crossing. Entering a welcoming pasture, a trod slants left up the bank towards Leyfield Farm. From a gate in the top corner turn right past the farm, with a fine barn, on an access track quickly out onto a road, Cattle Lane. Turn left for a few minutes to the start of trees on the left. Here a path crosses the open field on the right into Chantryhill Plantation. A clear path heads off left through the trees, along the bank to soon rise at the end into a field corner. Go left and head directly away with a line of trees on your right, a path forming with the road parallel below. At the end it runs between trees and modern buildings as a broader way back out onto Cattle Lane at the village edge. Go right on a footway to rejoin the main street alongside the bridge.

AROUND BARDSEY

*Delightful paths discover woodland crags and rich history
sandwiched in and amongst sleepy dormitory villages*

START *East Keswick (SE 360444; LS17 9EU)*

DISTANCE *7 miles (11¼km)*

ORDNANCE SURVEY 1:25,000 MAP
Explorer 289 - Leeds

ACCESS *Start from the village centre,
roadside parking. Leeds-Wetherby bus.*

    *East Keswick is the northernmost of a cluster of villages that
are distant rural satellites of the Leeds district. Its features
include the church of St Mary Magdalen and the Old Star and Duke
of Wellington pubs. An old roadsign stands at the junction outside
the old smithy: note the clock on an adjacent building.* From this
central junction descend the main street to the very bottom,
where a path runs between houses to a footbridge on Keswick
Beck. A surfaced path then rises between fields onto Rigton Lane,
where go right on the footway the short way to a junction. Rise left
a matter of yards before turning right at a gate onto the enclosed
bridleway of Gateon House Lane. This runs a splendid course with
good valley views before narrowing and emerging onto a rough
access road. Just a little further this ends at Gateon House, where
it narrows to rise through a slim, embowered section to meet

another broad track. Go right, again ending as another super way rises left, all the way over a brow and down onto Wike Lane.

Go left on the footway past houses then double back down a narrow lane to the right. Across a setted ford/footbridge, a lengthy pull up Spear Fir leads to a T-junction with Blackmoor Lane at the top. Go left on this broad ridge, a capacious verge giving way to a footway past straggling suburbia. Part way along take a hand-gate on the right between parallel driveways, and a good path runs an enclosed course that later broadens considerably. This same grassy way drops to the valley floor, and briefly up the other side. In front of a tall fence you join a track on the left alongside tall gates in front of a golf course. Don't pass through them but simply cross the track to follow an inviting path that slants up across a colourful bank beneath silver birches. Remaining outside a fence it runs on to emerge into a field at the end, then heads away enclosed to join a road on the edge of Scarcroft.

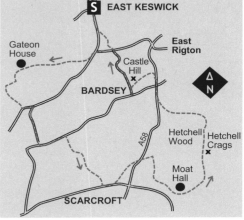

Go left into the village, but before the crossroads at the end (at a slight bend after Malthouse Close), bear left on an enclosed bridleway. *At the crossroads stands the Bracken Fox pub, while the contrastingly small tollhouse of 1826 still keeps an eye on the Leeds-Wetherby road.* The path runs through undergrowth and increasing greenery, finishing along a fieldside to a gate at the far end onto the A58. Cross and go a few strides left to a path heading away along a field-side to meet a track coming in from the left. At this point take a path rising right by the hedge. It crosses a small brow and drops to the very corner, delving into undergrowth and running left through greenery alongside a streamlet. Towards the end the path crosses a footbridge to emerge into a field: go left on the hedgeside to a wall-stile onto a driveway. Go left the few yards to the gates of Moat Hall, where your enclosed bridleway turns sharp right. It winds around outside a field to join Scarcroft Beck, which it soon bridges at the end before passing under a skewed railway bridge. *This stands on the Leeds-Wetherby line, closed in 1964 as a result of the Beeching cuts.* The path passes above an old works and then continues on past a very ruinous mill.

A little further you emerge into the colourful country of Pompocali. Keep to the left path rising gently into an area of heather knolls of recolonised quarries to your right. The path quickly forks as a grassy way drops left close by the stream. Yours keeps on beneath heathery slopes to quickly find several paths radiating. Either cross the brow in front or curve right between knolls, both quickly running to a path along the near side of trees ahead. In either case a path drops quickly through the trees to a bridle-gate onto a firm bridle-track. *This is largely on the course of a Roman road between Ilkley and York.* Drop left the short way towards a ford and footbridge, but take a kissing-gate on the right into Hetchell Wood, a Yorkshire Wildlife Trust reserve. A good path heads away, quickly espying Hetchell Crags just above. *This impressive facade offers climbers more than 50 named routes.*

Resume on the path to the end of the wood, with a small stream to the left. Emerging via a kissing-gate into a large field the path keeps to the left side, around a corner and into a second field to shortly enter trees. Remain on the main path which winds along to the old railway. Turn briefly right on its low embankment, then the path drops left off it to meet the A58 again. Cross and turn right on the footway past the junction at the edge of Bardsey, and a short way further take a surfaced path left into suburban Cornmill Close.

Rise a few strides past the attractive old cornmill on your right, and advance straight up a driveway to Bardsey Grange. *This was the birthplace in 1670 of Restoration dramatist William Congreve.* Don't enter but go left through a small gateway, and a path climbs to a fence at the top enclosing Castle Hill's ancient mound. *This grassy knoll is the well-defined site of a Norman motte and bailey: originally timber, the late 12th century stone castle of Adam de Bruce had but a brief existence.* Go left with the fence, the path becoming enclosed to run past the mound and onto Woodacre Lane opposite the village hall in Bardsey. *On your left is Callister Hall, a former school with a 1726 datestone.*

Bardsey is a leafy village greatly extended by modern housing. Just down to your left, enclosed within a lovely churchyard is All Hallows, boasting a splendid Anglo-Saxon tower, with other parts dating from Norman times. Just along the street from it is the Bingley Arms, one of several pubs claiming to be England's oldest as its origins date from AD 953. Despite being rebuilt down the centuries, it is said the older part has survived for over a thousand years: priest holes are secreted in the fireplace. Roughly halfway between Kirkstall Abbey and York, it was possibly a place to break journey for travelling monks. Turn up Woodacre Lane's footway past the school and out of the village, winding down to a T-junction with East Keswick just ahead. Go left a few strides to conclude on the surfaced fieldpath of your outward route.

Bardsey church

BARWICK IN ELMET

Easy paths to and from an absorbing, historic village

START *Scholes (SE 380364; LS15 4DH)*

DISTANCE *6¼ miles (10km)*

ORDNANCE SURVEY 1:25,000 MAP
Explorer 289 - Leeds

ACCESS *Start from main street near church
and pub, roadside parking. Bus from Leeds.*

From St Philip's modern church head east on the footway past
the Barley Corn pub, soon reaching a bend on the village edge.
Here a short access road runs left to allotments, continuing through
a gate as a grassy hedgeside cart track. This winds away, and on the
gentle brow of Limekiln Hill narrows to a path and passes through
the hedge to resume. Through a corner gap at the far end the path
runs briefly right to a kissing-gate, then resumes with the hedge on
your left. Running pleasantly along it trades sides at a corner, and
along a fieldside Barwick's church tower appears ahead. Becoming
enclosed by hedgerows it joins the head of suburban Carrfield Road.
Advance to Barwick's main street at the end, and turn left.

*Barwick in Elmet is a sizeable village recalling the ancient
kingdom of Elmet, and today is based around an immense maypole, the focus of triennial Spring Bank celebrations. Alongside is
a war memorial cross, with historic All Saints church close by. In*

addition to the Gascoigne Arms, Black Swan and New Inn, there is a deli/coffee house and a Post office/shop. Hall Tower Hill is the site of an Iron Age fort that over a millennium later was 'replaced' by a Norman motte and bailey of the de Lacys of Pontefract.

At the maypole go left a few yards along The Boyle alongside the Gascoigne Arms. Ahead is the short enclosed grassy pathway accessing Hall Tower Hill alongside a graveyard. The onward route turns right past a Methodist chapel, and the road winds around before dropping down to a tiny green where it swings left as Rakehill Road on the village edge. Here bear right down a short access road that ends just before a ford and footbridge on tiny Rake Beck. Across, a grassy hedgerowed way rises away, but oddly the right of way takes a gap on the right to run a parallel course up the fieldside. On the brow the adjacent track ends and the path continues down the hedgeside. At the bottom cross to a track in front of tiny Potterton Beck, crossed by a wooden footbridge.

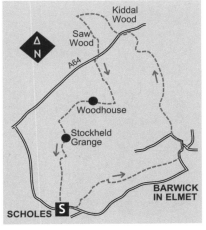

From a stile behind the bridge a thin path runs a delightful course through a narrow pasture between streamlet and hedge, on through several intervening stiles in lovely surrounds. At the far end you arrive beneath the A64 at Kiddal Bridge. Over a stile the path runs left through scrub below the road to emerge onto it. Cross with care to the start of the popular Red Bus Cafe lay-by. Here take a bridle-gate into Kiddal Wood, and a splendid, broad path heads away to arrive at a path junction at the far side.

Go left here on a path remaining inside the wood edge. Possibly initially muddy, it quickly improves to run to another path junction at another corner. Ignoring the cart track in front, take a clear path doubling back left into the trees. This runs a sustained, level course through Saw Wood, ignoring a couple of less inviting tracks going left. Ultimately reaching a massive hollow on your left, the path broadens and swings right. Leave it here for the onward thinner continuation, rising slightly to quickly arrive at the wood edge in front of the A64. Cross with even greater care on this less than ideal bend opposite the former Flying Horse Farm.

Go briefly right on the broad verge to a wall-stile on the left. Head directly away, reaching intermittent trees and roughly parallel telegraph poles. An old hedge soon encourages steps along its right side down to a drain and stile in the bottom. Bear left up this large arable field to an isolated guidepost at a path junction just short of the brow. Go right, the path leading directly to Woodhouse Farm. Cross a yard to a gate with a large, new house on your right. Advance straight on the driveway heading away to quickly reach a drive junction. Hear bear left to Whinmoor Nook just in front. Passing well to the right, it continues as an enclosed track to a T-junction with Stockheld Lane on the edge of Scholes.

Go left the few minutes to colourful Stockheld Grange Farm, and bear right into the yard. Passing between a stone barn and the house, head away on another access road ascending between

hedgerows. This runs on to a T-junction with the very broad, unsurfaced Rake Hill Road. Go briefly right and escape left through a kissing-gate into sports fields. Head away with a hedge on your left to a corner stile out, and continue on a broad grassy way through an arable field centre. From the stile ahead the path bears right across a pleasant pasture to the next stile, then left along the hedgeside to neighbouring stiles at the end. A short grassy way puts you back onto Main Street in Scholes.

Barwick in Elmet

ROUNDHAY PARK

*Lakes, gardens and woodland in a famous city park
with good paths out and back to a colourful village*

START *Roundhay (SE 336372; LS8 2LE)*

DISTANCE *5¹4 miles (8¹2km)*

ORDNANCE SURVEY 1:25,000 MAP
Explorer 289 - Leeds

ACCESS *Start from car park off Wetherby Road
alongside St John's church. Leeds-Wetherby bus.*

Roundhay is an up-market northerly suburb of Leeds, a century
ago home to the wealthier of Leeds merchants. Focal point is the
second largest city park in Europe – though in truth open country
sits to two sides of it. The estate was created by Thomas Nicholson
in the early 19th century, and acquired for the people of Leeds in
1871. The extensive Waterloo Lake is supported by the compact
Upper Lake, along with the restored Mansion House of 1826 and
gardens galore. Tropical World is a paying attraction housing a large
collection of plants and wildlife. Some of rock music's biggest
names have given concerts in the park, including the Rolling
Stones, Bruce Springsteen and U2. Near the southern entrances are
a tall clock tower of 1905 and the attractive Nicholson's
Almshouses of 1837 (now a school), with St John's church built by
the Nicholson Family of Roundhay Park in 1826.

Leave the car park by a regular path at an information board on the right, slanting up through trees to quickly gain the grassy dam of Waterloo Lake. *This is a lovely moment with the extensive former boating lake outspread.* Joining a firmer path, turn right along the shore beneath a wooded bank. Entering the more densely wooded upper reach, you arrive at a path junction at its head. Ignore that going left over the inflowing stream, and keep straight on. Within a minute you arrive alongside a stone-arched bridge on the inflowing stream. You shall return to this after the Shadwell loop, so for now ignore it and the continuing path, and instead turn right on the broad path rising away through the trees.

This immediately absorbs a lesser, earlier path from the right, and ascends pleasantly before easing out to reach a tiny section of solid wall at a path crossroads. Pass through the old gateway in front and resume through hollies, quickly emerging onto Leeds golf course. Cross this slender strip into another belt of trees, then across a broader fairway to a few corner trees where you join a broader way. *This is part of an ancient way from Leeds out to Harewood, and is soon in evidence again before you reach Shadwell.* Turn left here for a splendid stride on this well-defined green way across the last section of the course, and at the far side a few trees

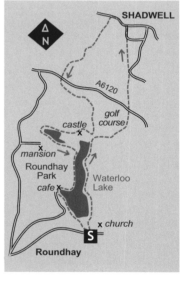

hide a stile onto the A6120 Leeds ring road.

Cross with care and head straight off on a hedgeside cart track. After a slight rise it runs on to the bend of Gateland Lane by a house on the outskirts of Shadwell. Don't follow it but take the enclosed rough road of Colliers Lane on your left, rising slightly and ending as a drive swings left. Advance straight on a super enclosed path, partly alongside Pitts Wood. *This proves a very atmospheric, hollowed section of the ancient road.* Just beyond the wood it emerges onto a suburban street: keep straight on past community herb beds to reach Shadwell's main street. *This linear village extends far to the right, featuring St Paul's church, a pinfold, a chippy in a house with a 1637 datestone, and a library/café in a former Methodist Chapel of 1814.* Turn left past the Red Lion pub and the Post office/shop, and just a couple of minutes further a small gate on the left sends a firm path off alongside a cornfield. This runs a splendid, unfailing course, sometimes enclosed, some-times fieldside, sometimes in trees, at the end emerging back onto the A6120.

Across, a path slants left the short way down to a junction at a stone-arched bridge on a streamlet. Don't cross but remain on the path running through Great Heads Wood, crossing the stream numerous times before settling down to run with it on your right. Only dropping ever slightly as it runs on through this valley, you will eventually reach the small stone bridge from earlier in the walk. Turning right across it, the broad path climbs away through trees, with a large grassy area just over to the left. Soon levelling out, ignore a level right branch and bear left, quickly arriving at an impressive restored folly known as The Castle.

Beyond it the path rises slightly and runs on to quickly emerge in front of the Upper Lake with its fountain. Take the path along its right shore, around the head and then forking. The surfaced right branch rises to a car park and road end at The Mansion (refreshments), while your way remains on the lakeside path. At its far end go left, and as it winds down through trees, leave almost at once on a path that immediately expires in extensive grass slopes. Simply drop straight down it onto a firm path on the western shore of Waterloo Lake. Turn right on this, soon emerging from trees into the open and curving around to a swan-filled corner at the Lakeside café. Passing between it and a car park, keep left on the broad, surfaced Carriage Drive that resumes above the lakeshore, soon arriving back at the dam. Again don't cross but immediately after it bear left off the carriageway on a hard path that winds down through trees to swing left parallel with the road to quickly arrive back at the start.

ECCUP RESERVOIR

Very easy reservoir circuit with spacious views

START *Adel (SE 280402; LS16 8DW)*

DISTANCE *6¹4 miles (10km)*

ORDNANCE SURVEY 1:25,000 MAP
Explorer 289 - Leeds **or**
Explorer 297 - Lower Wharfedale & Washburn Valley

ACCESS *Start from Adel Woods car park (unsigned but on map) on Stair Foot Lane, a third of a mile east of church.*

Leave by a path slanting up through trees on the opposite side of the road: avoiding any branches you quickly reach a bridle-gate at the wood edge. A good path curves right around the fieldside, becoming broader in the far corner to run a pleasant, enclosed course past Headingley golf course onto a road, King Lane, by King Lane Farm. Cross over and head away along a nice hedgerowed path to a stile into a field. *Ahead is a first glimpse of Eccup Reservoir beyond its plantations.* Keep straight on gently down the fieldside to a corner stile at the end. From it rise left with a fence over a brow and down to a stile onto another path outside a plantation corner. You shall return to this point after the reservoir circuit.

Turn right, still outside the trees on a super grassy path along the edge of this vast sheep pasture with glimpses of the lake. At the far end a small gate puts a firmer enclosed path into the edge of the trees, quickly reaching Reservoir Lodge. Ignore the drive and go straight ahead, finally getting close to the reservoir. A broad, firm path heads off with a fence, and remains so all the way to the dam. Despite the fence this is a nice and popular stroll, with woods on your right and spacious waters to your left. After a small inlet at the start a straighter stretch heads off, a deeper inlet intervening to deflect you around it to emerge just short of a parking area by the dam. *Eccup Reservoir was constructed in 1897, and stores water from the Washburn Valley reservoirs and the River Ouse. Big views across the water give a sense of the scale of the place.*

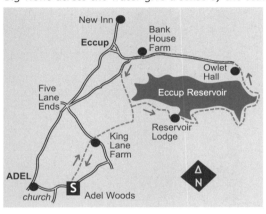

Go left on the dam road. Across, as the road rises right, almost at once take a bridle-gate on the left after two neighbouring driveways. An enclosed path rises to meet another drive at the top side of the houses at Owlet Hall.

This heads away to quickly meet a surfaced access road. Bear left for a long, straight stroll with good open views past hedgerows, and glimpses of the reservoir down to the left.

Towards the end Bank House Farm is passed, with an option to detour to the New Inn. When the road forks on the edge of scattered Eccup, bear left down to bridge Eccup Beck in trees and up the other side. Beyond a ruin on a brow the road drops past a lay-by, just past which a path is signed through a gate/stile on the left. A clear track heads away with a hedge, narrowing to a path. As the hedge turns off, rise over a gentle brow and down to a corner stile alongside the reservoir edge woods. The enclosed continuation rises to the path junction where you pick up the outward route. Simply retrace steps for the opening mile or so back to the start.

GOLDEN ACRE PARK

Leisurely walking between Adel and Bramhope

START *Bramhope (SE 266417; LS16 8BQ)*

DISTANCE *5³4 miles (9¹4km)*

ORDNANCE SURVEY 1:25,000 MAP
Explorer 297 - Lower Wharfedale & Washburn Valley

ACCESS *Start from Golden Acre Park car park on
A660 a mile south of Bramhope. Leeds-Otley bus.*

Leave the car park at the bottom corner, where a path runs
the few paces down steps to an underpass beneath the main road.
You shall finish through this, so for now advance on the bridge at
Breary Marsh, and a broad path ascends very gently into trees.
Rising the short way to a T-junction on the edge of the woodland,
bear right along the wood edge with a field to your left. Fully
entering trees, another junction is reached at a footbridge. Across
it take the broad path rising left alongside a streamlet to another
junction beneath the grassy embankment of Paul's Pond, a former
fishpond. A little path rises onto the embankment path just above.

Go left, tracing the same path round the entire pond, much of
it within woodland not by the shore. Coming back down the other
side, your path merges with the earlier one, and goes left through
a gate out into a field. The still firm path traces a hedgeside to Old
Rushes Farm, passing in and out of its grounds via bridle-gates -

though a path to the left avoids the grounds. Head away on its drive, swinging left alongside Marshes Plantation to Rushes Farm. Becoming surfaced, it continues out past a scout camp and swings right up onto Cookridge Lane on the edge of suburban Cookridge.

Cross and go left on the footway, crossing Green Lane and then re-crossing the main road on a zebra crossing. Head away left on the access road of Hall Lane, soon ending after houses on your left. A surfaced path briefly takes over to enter a car park at Cookridge Hall, a golf and country club. Advance straight on past a driving range to the main buildings, and keep on with them all on your right. At the end two golf tracks head away: after looking back to see the frontage of the hall take the right one, almost at once transforming into a nicer cart track between scrub. Further on it ends abruptly on re-entering the course.

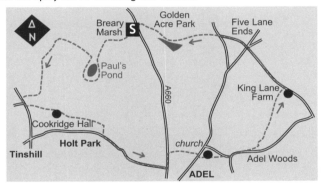

Keep on with trees on your left to a little brow where the track re-forms, dropping to a cross-paths with a golf track, and on into hummocky grassland. Just yards further a sign indicates a thinner, clear path branching right the short way to a fence at Holt Farm, where another golf track runs left outside the grounds. Almost at once this swings left to remain on the course, but a normal path keeps straight on into trees to emerge onto Holt Lane. Go left as it winds leafily around to the edge of suburban Holt Park. A gate on the left sends a parallel firm path along a wood edge, soon rejoining the road in suburbia. Bear left on this estate road through open grassy areas then on to the A660 at the Lawnswood Arms.

Go left on the footway past the pub, and after the housing opposite ends, quickly reaching a stone gatepost. Cross with care to a path through an old wall and off through a field centre. After an old stile it rises gently across a similar field to a stile onto Church Lane. Cross straight over into Adel churchyard, where a flagged path runs to the church. *Adel is at the northernmost limits of Leeds suburbia, with a wealth of lovely rural corners. Best feature is St John the Baptist's church in this peaceful spot: largely from the mid 12th century with a resplendent doorway, it was described by the noted historian Nikolaus Pevsner as one of the best and most complete Norman village churches in Yorkshire.*

The path continues past the church and out the other side: at a small gate you enter an access road between two nice older houses. Advance straight on, a path taking over to rapidly emerge onto Back Church Lane opposite York Gate Garden. *This award-winning garden boasts a wealth of fascinating features neatly crammed into its single acre: it also has a tearoom.* Bear right on the footway outside the gardens to a T-junction, going left on leafy Stair Foot Lane. This drops down out of suburbia to stone-arched Stair Foot Bridge on tiny Adel Beck. Immediately across, ignore a gate on the left and take a path rising gently left into trees. Rapidly forking, bear gently left to rise through curious winding ways in the trees to meet a wider path rising from a car park down to your right. Go

left, avoiding any branches to quickly reach a bridle-gate at the edge of the wood. A good path curves right around the fieldside, becoming broader in the far corner. It runs a pleasant, enclosed course past Headingley golf course to emerge onto a road, King Lane, alongside King Lane Farm.

Cross and go left on a welcome footway to aptly-named Five Lane Ends. *On the left is a stone guidepost inscribed with hands pointing to Chapeltown and Adel.* Continue straight on King Lane's footway the short way to its junction with Arthington Road, and go straight across on a firm path on the edge of a strip of woodland. Within a minute you are within the grounds of Golden Acre Park, so cross into the open green spaces to your right. Just short of a stone-arched bridge bear right to a path junction at an information panel. Go left on the broad, hard path which runs above the nearby lakeshore to the hub of the park.

Spacious Golden Acre Park is a hugely popular amenity, with a splendid arboretum and gardens, and a lake and rich woodland. Here also are a tearoom, shop and WC. Opened in 1932 as a pleasure park with boating, swimming pool, fairground attractions, zoo and a mile-long miniature railway, this existence was short-lived, and after some derelict years its present guise was established by Leeds City Council in the 1940s. A small section of the old railway survives alongside your path. Beyond the café the main path swings left to run briefly parallel beneath the main road to reach the underpass back to the car park.

Opposite: Adel church

Golden Acre Park

WHARFE VALLEY

Panoramic Wharfedale views linking two villages

START *Bramhope (SE 248432; LS16 9AX)*

DISTANCE *5³⁄4 miles (9¹⁄4km)*

ORDNANCE SURVEY 1:25,000 MAP
Explorer 297 - Lower Wharfedale & Washburn Valley

ACCESS *Start from the village centre. Car park
on Old Lane behind pub. Leeds-Otley bus.*

Bramhope is a substantial village whose characterful centre
sits amid extensive suburbia. At the heart is the Cross, watched
over by the Fox & Hounds pub (with a 1728 lintel), old cottages,
shops, bakery and a chippy. The cross itself incorporates a lantern
and four fingerposts, the present one of 1936 having replaced a
19th century one. The village centre was by-passed as long ago as
1842 by the Leeds-Otley turnpike, the present main road. From the
Cross turn north past the pub, descending Church Hill to the main
road. On the right is the modest church of St Giles dating from
1881, and on the junction outside is a grand old milestone of 1850,
with distances to assorted destinations in miles and furlongs. Cross
and go left past the Britannia Hotel entrance to the Puritan Chapel.
Erected around 1649 by the Dyneley family of Bramhope Hall, it is
one of only a handful built during Cromwell's Commonwealth.
Restored in 1966, it is open to view on Sundays, Easter to October.

Just yards further, bear right on Staircase Lane. *The 'staircase' is the steep ascent this old lane makes from Pool on the valley floor, in use since monastic times.* As it drops down, take an iron kissing-gate on the right immediately after the houses. *You are greeted by a super vista over the Wharfe Valley, featuring Almscliff Crag, Kirkby Overblow and Arthington church spire.* Slant down to the far corner, and through another such gate turn right along the hedgeside. At the end the path becomes enclosed to emerge into another pasture. A grassy track slants down a hollow at Broom Bank, bearing right to its tapering conclusion. Here a grassy track passes through a gate/stile to run parallel with the railway.

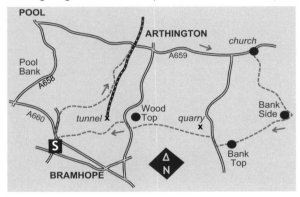

The Leeds-Harrogate line has just emerged from the wooded confines of Bramhope Tunnel, completed in 1849 with a castellated portal, and one of the network's longer tunnels at more than two miles. Workers who toiled during its construction are remembered by a memorial in a corner of Otley parish church, which replicates the tunnel entrance. Remain on the track until an underpass in the rail embankment, turning through it to continue on a now enclosed track. *Immediately on your left but sadly now blocked by fencing, until recent times an old red-brick building still bore the name 'Arthington'. A relic of the days when this was a triangle of routes, this was Arthington Junction station until its 1965 closure. In fact, the line you've just passed beneath is not the present one, but the curve of the old Otley branch, a victim of Dr Beeching's axe.*

The track emerges onto a broad access road with the surviving line in front. Turn left on this beneath another rail bridge, the third side of the triangle. As Station Road this runs on to meet the A659 at Arthington, directly opposite the Wharfedale. *Arthington's pub (originally the Station Hotel) is the first of this straggling village's features, the last being your objective, the church.* In the absence of alternatives here begins a mile-long road walk, tempered by a 40mph speed limit and, crucially, an unbroken footway.

Cross to the footway and turn right under the rail bridge. *Keen eyes will discern the church spire ahead. The walk highlights both the great length of Arthington, and various historic aspects. En route you pass a converted Methodist chapel, the former Post office and a turnpike milestone. Across the valley, meanwhile, Almscliff Crag and the Wharfedale Viaduct make a prominent pair. Further, you pass the old schoolhouse of 1872, the architectural oddity of Crag View, the village hall with Victorian postbox, and a lodge at the entrance to Arthington Hall across from an old West Riding roadsign at the foot of the road to Adel.* A little beyond the Adel junction you reach the church. *Dating from 1864 and dominated by the impressively tall spire, it is the work of famous architect Giles Gilbert Scott. In 2007 its redundancy saw it 'change faith' from St Peter's to the Coptic Orthodox church of St Mary & St Abanoub.*

The road is left by a wall-stile on the right immediately before the church, running outside the churchyard wall to a stile onto an enclosed track. Turn left, past the rear of the church and vicarage, then turning sharp right and narrowing to a path along the side of horse paddocks. Through a gate at the end continue on a further fieldside to another gate, then bear left across a grassy pasture. Passing an outer corner of Blanket Wood (omitted from, yet named on, the map), cross to the far corner, and from the small gate ascend a steep field outside another wood. From a stile in a fence rising above the wood, ascend to pass left of Bank Side's farmhouse wall, and on to a fence-stile accessing its drive just below a junction.

Turn right on the super track of Bank Top Lane rising gently away. *Used by the Ebor Way long distance path, it gives extensive views over the Wharfe Valley, from moors west of the Washburn Valley around to Almscliff Crag.* Rising ever gently it transforms into a narrower old way between foliage, becoming enclosed by undergrowth before levelling out to run on between old walls. Later broadening into a farm track it passes left of the buildings at former Bank Top Farm to emerge onto Black Hill Road. Turn briefly right just as far as the end of the field on your left, where a bridle-way enters a belt of woodland above the rim of Arthington Quarry. *Though largely screened, its golden sandstone walls are well seen at one point.* Eventually emerging through a bridle-gate at the end, head directly away on a field boundary. Soon absorbing an access track, advance along this all the way to emerge onto a back road.

Turn right, descending a short way until the end of woodland on the left. Now go left on a bridleway outside the wood bottom before delving deep into trees at the end. As a broader way it runs on through the wood, soon rising between gardens to emerge into an up-market suburb. Cross straight over the road and rise on an enclosed way, emerging onto a second such road. Do likewise again, up onto a third street. With no way ahead now, turn right, and as it winds up at the end, take a good path into trees on the right. This ascends between gardens and woodland to emerge back onto the A660 opposite the church. *On the left are surviving remains of the restored Town Well.* Re-cross the road (with great care on this bend) to return up Church Hill to the village centre.

The Fox & Hounds, Bramhope

LEEDS-LIVERPOOL CANAL

A super towpath trod with history, woodland and riverbank

START *Kirkstall (SE 259354; LS5 3BT)*

DISTANCE *6^{1}2 miles (10^{1}2km)*

ORDNANCE SURVEY 1:25,000 MAP
Explorer 288 - Bradford & Huddersfield

ACCESS *Start from Wyther Lane car park immediately off Broad Lane just across river at Kirkstall Bridge. Numerous bus services including Leeds, Keighley, Pudsey, Halifax.*

Kirkstall is renowned for the impressive remains of its abbey, founded by Cistercian monks in 1152 in a lovely setting by the Aire. Its dark gritstone contrasts with the softer tones of rural Dales establishments, none of which witnessed the industrial age that gripped Kirkstall. The abbey is setting for various events, while Abbey House Museum occupies a monastic gatehouse. The Leeds-Liverpool Canal runs a 127^{1}4-mile course between its two great city termini, the northernmost of three trans-Pennine waterways. Its engineers took advantage of the low-level Aire Gap to breach the Pennines by way of a chain of locks, only resorting to tunnelling for a mile-long stretch at Foulridge on the Lancashire border. Begun in 1770, it fully opened in 1816 for what proved to be a short-lived industrial use, being swiftly overtaken by the railways. Today it is a vibrant amenity for all manner of leisure users.

Join the adjacent towpath of the Leeds-Liverpool Canal and turn right on hollowed flags under Kirkstall Brewery Bridge. Alongside is the first of several milestones, while on the opposite bank is the former Kirkstall Brewery. *This began over 200 years ago as a maltings, becoming a brewery in 1833 and survived takeovers for 150 years until closure by Whitbreads in 1983: it is now student accommodation.* A weekday community café in the woods precedes the B6157 road bridge. Emerging into open countryside, almost at once the abbey appears over to your right. Passing Kirkstall Little Lock, the towpath ambles on to the triple staircase of Forge Locks. *Kirkstall Forge just across the river was a major complex dating from the 18th century, on the site of a bloomery for iron smelting operated by the monks. A long and illustrious history ended in 2003, and a new railway station opened on the site in 2016, over a century after its predecessor closed.*

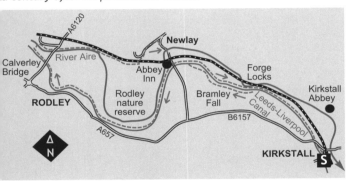

Whilst you could simply remain on the towpath, ideally enjoy a spell in the adjacent woodland of Bramley Fall. Cross the bridge on the top lock and a small footbridge over the surplus flow alongside into the trees, then immediately turn right to commence a canalside walk on a regular path. Ignoring any early branches, the path runs a grand course by the water's edge. *Minor caution is needed in a couple of places if wet, while above you are hummocks of old quarries which provided stone for Stanley Ferry aqueduct in WALK 13.* Further on, just after a towpath milestone opposite, a left fork quickly meets a wider path running beneath a distinct embankment. This leads into an open area with Newlay Locks just ahead. At the end of the grass, a few yards back into trees leads to the staircase of three at Newlay Locks. Cross a tiny footbridge over the overflow and a bridge on the top lock to rejoin the towpath for the two minutes further to the road bridge under Pollard Lane.

Just down to your right the Abbey Inn awaits, but you shall return to that later. For now, pass under the bridge and continue along the towpath all the way to Calverley Bridge. After a busy moorings you pass intriguing Whitecote House and on through largely open terrain. Another milestone precedes a second swing-bridge with an option to visit Rodley nature reserve. Continuing, the next milestone stands opposite the Rodley Barge pub on the opposite bank just before another swing bridge at colourful Rodley Moorings. Just two minutes further beneath the concrete Horsforth Road Bridge you arrive at Calverley Bridge (though not the bridge itself quite yet), a busy spot featuring the Railway pub and a shed café.

Leaving the towpath take the rough road past the pub, quickly narrowing as it slants down to Calverley Bridge on the River Aire. *Rebuilt in 1775 it was a toll bridge until a century ago, and its setted surface makes a delightful pedestrian crossing. Across it stood Calverley & Rodley Station, a victim of the Beeching cuts in 1965.*

Across it take the right-hand path dropping slightly to follow the river downstream. Rejoining the higher path it passes beneath the modern road bridge to commence a splendid stride through open countryside. On reaching a wooded bank where the river swings right, the path rises left through the wood edge to a kissing-gate, then up a fieldside. With a wood on your left and good open views, the path runs on above a deep railway cutting. A kissing-gate sends the path along a brief, enclosed course above the railway. Quickly ending at a rail bridge, a track crosses the bridge to emerge onto suburban Newlaithes Road. Turn right on here, and just short of the junction at the end a short-cut setted path drops right to turn down Newlay Lane to Newlay Bridge on the river.

Plaques on either side of this iron pedestrian bridge proudly announce that this former toll bridge was erected by John Pollard of Newlay House in 1819, as was the surviving tollhouse on the near side. Across, rise to cross the railway bridge to finally arrive at the homely Abbey Inn. *Newlay Station here was another victim of the Beeching cuts.* Opposite the pub a path leaves a driveway heading off, slanting up through trees to quickly rejoin the canal towpath. Turn left the short way back to Newlay Locks and this time remain on the towpath to pick up the outward route at Forge Locks, to finish along the towpath as you began. Between the two sets of locks you pass another milestone.

Opposite: Kirkstall Abbey  *At Forge Locks*

AIRE VALLEY

A splendid waterside ramble from riverbank to towpath

START *Calverley Bridge (SE 221367; LS13 1NR)*

DISTANCE *5 miles (8km)*

ORDNANCE SURVEY 1:25,000 MAP
Explorer 288 - Bradford & Huddersfield

ACCESS *Start from a popular canalside parking area just beneath A6120 ring-road bridge. Horsforth-Pudsey bus.*

The start point features a tiny café in a shed. Saving the canal for the return, begin by bearing right away from the towpath along a rough road past houses to the Railway pub. Continue past it down an old road to the 'real' Calverley Bridge on the River Aire. *Rebuilt in 1775, it was a toll bridge until a century ago, and now makes an excellent pedestrian crossing.* Across, advance a few steps to a path junction just before reaching a road, then turn left on a few steps down into a riverside pasture. Head upstream beneath a pylon, with modern housing to the right. The tapering field puts you on a better riverbank path, though the housing continues for some time. The path passes through an arched tunnel beneath double railway bridges, and pleasantly on for some time until deflected away from the river by a wall to meet a broader path. Go left on this wallside way beneath a large field. Broadening, it emerges at a surfaced waterworks road-end by a lone house. Drop left a few strides and outside the garden edge into a field, where a firm path heads off along the foot of Cragg Wood, soon arriving back on the riverbank.

A delightful section is now enjoyed, opening out with nice views and good river scenery. Further, the path passes beneath Woodhouse Bridge, a massive railway viaduct, and then on past sports fields to lead all the way onto the A658 at Rawdon Meadows car park at Apperley Bridge. Go right to cross at an island, then with the Stansfield Arms to your right, go left on Apperley Road the short way to cross Apperley Bridge itself. *Dating from the late 18th century, a barely decipherable inscribed tablet adorns its crest.* Across, turn left past the George & Dragon back to the main road, and go right to re-cross at pedestrian lights.

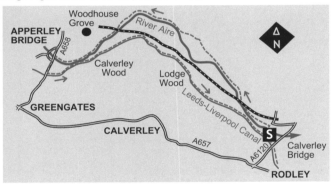

Turn right on the footway, and ignoring Parkin Lane, rise to a bridge where drop left down steps onto the Leeds-Liverpool Canal towpath. *The canal is featured in WALK 24.* Head away left between new houses, and on beneath Calverley Cutting bridge. *This carries the Thornhill family's Calverley Cutting of 1856, which replaced an old packhorse track through Calverley Wood.* After a string of moored barges the towpath leads grandly on with much woodland and later open pastures. Initially the Aire itself provides company, and the surroundings open out further at Lodge Swing Bridge after woodland ends just after a second milestone. Ultimately you will return unfailingly to your starting point. Two minutes further under the modern road bridge is Rodley Moorings with boats, a public area, and the Rodley Barge pub just over the swing bridge.

Aberford